Dedication

For my mother, Rita, who always let us check out as many books as we wanted, and who is the only person I know who has read *Gone with the Wind* in one sitting.

Acknowledgments

Special thanks go to: My friends at St. Louis County Library, especially the fantastic staff at my branch: Annie Fuller, Marcia Green, Jerry Huth, Richard McAfee, Jessica Engle, Susan Hackmann, Anita Hutkin, Marquitta Parnell, Laura Simon, Mary Walter, Barb Wexler, Chris Carter, Betty McMahan, Jessica Nations, Kara Toenjes, Andrew Bono, and Joe Montgomery. You keep me inspired and on my toes.

Sabrina, Chris, and Riley Lunn, for all of the love; Erin Magner, for all of the laughs; Alvin and Ariana DiLibero Schopp, for cabin adventures and the best sort of friendship.

The friends who provided ideas for these booklists, particularly: Josh Zink, Tari Simpson, Sarajane Alverson, Ellen Coy, Caleb Coy, Heidi Ardizzone, Conrad Rader, Britta Krabill, Kathleen Smith, Amy Burger, Kelly Bono, Jennifer Hall, Adam Rosen, Lizz Jensen, and Susannah Eisenbraun.

The fabulous folks at Adams Media, especially Tom Hardej, who has a knack for putting me at ease.

Agent and friend Kate McKean, for being such a positive influence in my life.

My neighbors in Old North St. Louis, for making me feel perfectly at home.

The staff at La Mancha Coffeehouse, for feeding me the best waffles in the city as I wrote.

The Unorthodox Book Club for Extraordinary Women, for the Sunday afternoons together. (I'm sure you'll recognize many of the titles listed in this book!)

Sarina, Daniel, Jayson, Kendra, Mom, and Dad. Our family may be weirder than others, but that's why I love you so.

Travis, for effortless love, laughter, and adventure, always.

Contents

Introduction

If you're looking for a literary love affair, you're in luck. In this book, you'll find the 200 coolest, best, and most important books I've come across in my years as a reader and librarian. From the sometimes-somber books about the American Dream fallacy, to a list of fantastic graphic biographies and memoirs, to young adult books that adults can really get into, *Check These Out* is a checklist of books that I highly recommend to any reader. These are the books I pull out when someone asks for a quick recommendation, a "good book" in a world filled to the brim with great, and not-so-great, things to read. This is not meant to be a stand-in for what those in Library Land consider typical readers' advisory—a fundamental library service that fosters an ongoing relationship between a librarian and a library patron. This book does not operate on the principle "if you like book A, you'll like book B"; rather, this book offers an intimate glimpse at the bedtime reading on my nightstand, the books that line my shelves, and the stories that have highlighted my career in library science.

Choosing the titles in the following fifteen lists was a fun challenge. I scoured my Goodreads page and old reading journals. I finally got around to many of the titles on my ever-growing "to read" list. I compared notes with fellow readers I trust. I was reminded about books I'd loved at different places in my life. Committing to these titles is like entering into a relationship. Rediscovering some of them was like seeing an old friend unexpectedly. These are the genres that intrigue me the most as a librarian, and each chapter includes a diverse mix of titles, authors, and publication dates.

You'll find check-mark boxes next to each title, and there is an alphabetical list of all of the titles at the back of the book. For those of you who are checking this out from the library, whatever you do, please don't write in the book! Your friendly neighborhood librarian will hear about it from a disgruntled patron and then will have to spend several minutes apologizing for humanity. Please see my website (*www.ginasheridan.com*) for a printable version of the checklist instead.

This book will help you discover or rediscover a favorite story and inspire you to keep a list of your own or share one that you've created. Let it lead you to your local library to get a personalized reading suggestion, or rile you up because I've neglected to include one of your favorite titles or genres—when these things happen, we all win. Because we are reading, talking about, and sharing books.

So, pull out your "to read" list, turn on your e-reader, get out your library card. Start checking out books and checking them off.

Chapter 1

American't Dream

*Stories about trying, and failing,
to get ahead in America.*

Dusty trails out West to Wall Street riches to a
picture-perfect home in a suburban cul-de-sac.
Stories about America are often romanticized—
they are filled with roads paved with gold, prom-
ises of freedom, limitless riches bubbling over
the top of a melting pot of dreams fulfilled. We
tend to glom on to the stories of the underdog
succeeding: those miraculous, one-in-a-million
tales of utter success. Why? Because we des-
perately want to believe those stories not only
exist but are the norm. That we, too, can attain
complete and utter success, or at least make
our neighbors believe we have. That if we work

hard, keep our chins up, and follow all the rules, we can embody the dream. But the books on this list illustrate the goings on in the shadows of the American dream. These are the stories of people trying and failing to clear the enormous obstacles they face. Packed with crazy confrontations, cultural clashes, and raw humanity, these books are about the people who don't fit in and, try as they might, just can't get ahead in America.

◻ *The Beautiful Things That Heaven Bears* (2007)
by Dinaw Mengestu

• • • • • •

Sepha Stephanos is an Ethiopian American running a drab grocery store in a poor section of Washington, D.C. When a white
woman moves into the neighborhood with her ten-year-old
biracial daughter, Sepha is first confused by their presence in
the neighborhood but is soon taken with them. What strikes
me most about this story of an Ethiopian immigrant's search for
success, peace, and acceptance on a continent that does not feel
like home is the sheer matter-of-factness of the narrative. This
is not a story filled with twists and turns; it's a genuine representation of the everyday of unbelonging. We've all felt out of
place somewhere or sometime. Mengestu helps me understand
how much more this feeling is amplified for a person new to the
United States.

◻ *Black Like Me* (1961)
by John Howard Griffin

••••••

Growing up in the racially divided city of St. Louis taught me that the issues surrounding social and racial inequality often go unspoken but noticed, unacknowledged but reinforced. This book, about one journalist's exploration of racial inequality, may have been published decades ago, but recent events in the United States have shown that it is not at all dated.

I've always been fascinated by stories about racial "passing," stories usually told from an African American's perspective on passing as white. In *Black Like Me*, white journalist John Howard Griffin passes as black. Griffin, who sought to experience what it is like to be on the receiving end of racial discrimination, used dermatological drugs and ultraviolet lamps to darken his skin in order to pose as a black man traveling across the South for six weeks in 1959. He immediately noticed a stark and distinct change in the way white store clerks, bus drivers, law enforcement officials, women, and men treated him. Although he did not encounter violence, he was refused service, had trouble finding work, and was routinely asked about his genitals and sexual experiences because of bizarre stereotypes about African-American men. Although the book is distressing, the *Washington Post* book critic Jonathan Yardley wrote that *Black Like Me* "awoke significant numbers of white Americans to truths about discrimination of which they had been unaware or had denied."

The project and its backlash resulted in the near-death beating of Griffin and sparked a temporary move to Mexico in order to protect his family. Fittingly, the title is the last line of the poem "Dream Variations" by Langston Hughes. For further reading from the African-American perspective on the topic of racial "passing," also check out *A Chosen Exile: A History of Racial Passing in American Life* (2014) by Allyson Hobbs and *Passing* (1929) by Nella Larsen, a classic novel included in Chapter 11: Too Cool for School.

◻ *Give Me My Father's Body:*
The Life of Minik, the New York Eskimo (1986)
by Kenn Harper

••••••

In this unbelievable account of exploitation and exile, famed explorer Robert Peary brings six-year-old Inuit Minik and others from Greenland to New York in 1897 as a sort of show-and-tell, and then abandons the child when the rest of the party, including Minik's father, falls ill with tuberculosis. As if that's not shocking enough, Minik later learns that his father's body is on display—owned—by the American Museum of Natural History. Minik's fight to bring his father's body home for a proper burial and his struggle to assimilate in America, or to return to Greenland, leaves him lost, alone, and devastated. Almost 100 years after the injustice and scientific arrogance that shaped Minik's life took place, author Kenn Harper played a role in pressuring the museum to finally return the Inuit remains to Greenland. Actor and producer Kevin Spacey was so moved by Minik's story that he wrote the foreword to the 2001 edition of the book and optioned the film rights. Minik's story is chilling, sad, and an important account of the exploitation of indigenous people by the scientific community.

☐ *González and Daughter Trucking Co.: A Road Novel with Literary License* (2005) by María Amparo Escandón

••••••

Listing this book in the American't Dream category is partially cheating, as it's mostly set in a Mexican prison for female inmates. In the story, Libertad tells her fellow inmates and Library Club members the tale of Joaquín, a former literature professor and Mexican fugitive trying to make a go at life in the United States as a truck driver while raising his daughter on the road. Joaquín is a complicated, paranoid, possessive man who protects his daughter almost to a fault, and often lands the pair in precarious situations. The story of Joaquín and his daughter not only captivates the other inmates and inspires them to bond with one another, but it eventually reveals the shocking act Libertad committed to land in prison. Reminiscent of the Netflix show *Orange Is the New Black*, this book includes bits and pieces of information about individual prison inmates and explores the redemptive power of storytelling.

The House on Mango Street (1984)
by Sandra Cisneros

●●●●●●

Mexican-American author Sandra Cisneros taught me about the beauty of vignettes. Short, poignant stories that could stand alone but instead are woven together to tell a sweeping tale that pulls together common themes and symbols—these make for perfect bathtub or nighttime reading. In *The House on Mango Street*, readers subtly and unassumingly follow the struggle of Esperanza Cordero, a Chicana girl who thinks her name sounds clunky. Esperanza tells it like it is, which means the stories are sometimes joyous, sometimes unknowingly heart-wrenching, as she describes the people and the Chicago she knows. "Bums in the Attic" is my favorite piece of writing of all time. The first time I read it was the first time I remember audibly gasping while reading. Also look for Cisneros's books of poetry, *My Wicked Wicked Ways* (1987) and *Loose Woman* (1994). If you have little ones, check out her children's books, too.

Last Night at the Lobster (2007)
by Stewart O'Nan

••••••

Stewart O'Nan manages to make the mundane extraordinary in this book about restaurant workers. The story begins as Manny DeLeon arrives for his last shift at the Red Lobster restaurant he manages on the last day before it closes forever because of lackluster business. Manny has tried his best to manage his employees while struggling with his own issues—finding himself in love with one of his waitresses, stressing over his pregnant girlfriend, grieving over his beloved grandmother's death, and worrying whether his employees like him or not. But now that his restaurant is closing, he's being moved to the Olive Garden and getting a demotion. When I was fifteen, I was desperate for spending money so I lied about my age in order to get a job at McDonald's. I'll never forget the cast of characters I worked with—the married guy who had an obvious crush on a girl half his age, the girl who dated every male employee who worked in the kitchen—the pranks we would play on each other, or the way we fiercely stood together against drunk or angry customers but sold each other out for extra shifts. O'Nan nails the life of a late-twentieth-century restaurant employee in America with this touching, realistic story.

The Namesake (2003)
by Jhumpa Lahiri

••••••

The Ganguli family settles in Cambridge, Massachusetts, from Calcutta, India. Husband and wife Ashoke and Ashima have different ways of coping with their new American life and soon have a son, Gogol, who grows up with his own set of struggles as a first-generation Indian American. Having to simultaneously experience two different cultures takes its toll on Gogol, who, for all the hope and expectations his parents have for him, pretty much turns out to be a jerk who can't understand or acknowledge his parents' perspective until it's too late. But what I love about this book is that we can all relate to Gogol's attitude. We all have things we learn too late and people we have taken for granted. Whenever people say they don't have regrets, I think, *Sheesh! Well, aren't you lucky?!* For other great reads on the American immigrant experience, look to Julia Alvarez (who is included in the "Very Truly Yours" chapter), Edwidge Danticat, Junot Díaz, and Anzia Yezierska.

◻ *Nickel and Dimed:*
On (Not) Getting By in America (2001)
by Barbara Ehrenreich

"What you don't necessarily realize when you start
selling your time by the hour is that what you're
actually selling is your life.*"*

●●●●●●

This book is a great way to begin a conversation about unequal pay and poverty in America. As long as you aren't looking to get an exhaustive look at socioeconomic disparity in the United States, and see it for what it is—proof that no one can live on minimum wage no matter how hard one works—you won't be disappointed. In this quick read, Ehrenreich moves to three cities and tries out several minimum-wage jobs: Walmart clerk, housekeeper, waitress, and nursing home attendant. She is self-critical for the entire journey, constantly keeping in mind she is only a researcher and therefore can only scratch the surface of what life is like for so many.

◻ *Revolutionary Road* (1961)
by Richard Yates

••••••

When we are young, society whispers into our ears that finding a decent spouse, buying a house in the suburbs, and having a couple of kids will make all of our dreams come true. *Revolutionary Road*, written just after American suburban development really took off in the 1950s, shows us it doesn't. In fact, when I first read this book as a teenager, it felt like the first time I had permission to question such social mores and really think about goals I wanted to attain for myself. See, the couple in this book suffers from the American dream malaise—co-dependent marriage, resentment, suburban ennui, and a life of boredom, becoming exactly the type of people they'd previously pitied and mocked.

◻ *Typical American* (1991)
by Gish Jen

• • • • • •

Not only do I appreciate Gish Jen's incredible writing, but I love that she goes by her nickname Gish, rather than her given name, Lillian. The author explains, "'Lillian' was a nice Chinese girl. 'Gish' was, shall we say, less well behaved." How glad I am that Gish is less well behaved, since she brings us stories like *Typical American*. Aside from several laugh-out-loud moments, the humor in this novel is ironic and wonderfully dry. The Changs—Ralph, his sister, Theresea, and his wife, Helen—come to America to wait out Communist control of China. They find themselves surrounded by "typical Americans," and know without a doubt that their traditional Chinese way of doing things is superior. Told with wit and empathy, readers learn alongside the Changs that "typical American" may be a misnomer, and that sometimes everything that can go wrong does go wrong.

Water for Elephants (2006)
by Sara Gruen

●●●●●●

One of my favorite reactions when something decidedly unfunny happens is "That was funny—like a circus to an elephant." Nothing good could possibly happen in a story that involves a circus, am I right? When orphaned Jacob Jankowski jumps a freight train during the Great Depression, he suddenly finds himself with the job of veterinarian for a traveling circus. He's thrust into a world of misfits, abuse, and murder. If Stephen King's *The Green Mile* (1996) and Kevin Baker's *Dreamland* (1999) had a circus baby, this book would be it. One of my favorite storytelling techniques is what I call looking-back-from-the-nursing-home, which is what instantly hooked me on *Water for Elephants*. Looking at the past with longing, love, and regret is something we can all relate to.

◻ *The Women of Brewster Place* (1982)
by Gloria Naylor

••••••

This 1983 National Book Award winner for First Novel is about a group of "gold," "saffron," "nutmeg," and "ebony" black women and their time spent living in Brewster Place—a collection of dilapidated, dirty tenements in an unnamed city. Not only are the women of the book tied to a place, but they also share the common experiences of being abandoned, having trouble with the men in their lives, and discovering strength within themselves. It's a great example of a setting-driven book, and I love how Naylor manages to turn Brewster Place into a hulking brute of a character itself. Also check out Naylor's companion book, *The Men of Brewster Place*, published sixteen years later.

⬜ *The Worst Hard Time:*
The Untold Story of Those Who Survived
the Great American Dust Bowl (2006)
by Timothy Egan

"Going to the outhouse was an ordeal, a wade through
shoulder-high drifts, forced to dig to make forward
progress."

●●●●●●

Before reading this National Book Award-winning book, I had no idea that American meteorologists rated the massive black blizzards of the 1930s Dust Bowl the number-one weather event of the twentieth century. In fact, I didn't know that the billows of dust were called "black blizzards" and some reached as far as New York City and Washington, D.C. Egan presents the causes of the crisis as well as various perspectives. I'm so grateful that Egan decided to seek out interviews with survivors of the Dust Bowl before these last witnesses passed on.

A Yellow Raft in Blue Water (1987)
by Michael Dorris

●●●●●●

A Yellow Raft in Blue Water, broken into three parts and told from the perspectives of women from the same troubled American Indian family, is a book that starts in the present and moves backward in time. The story begins with fifteen-year-old Rayona, a half-black, half–American Indian girl struggling to find herself and understand Christine, her detached mother. But Christine has her own troubles, torn between the various men in her life and wanting to leave the reservation for Seattle in the wake of the Vietnam War. And then there's Aunt Ida, the fierce, yet tender, matriarch of the family who has suffered her own hardships and fought to keep the family's secrets. Misunderstandings between the women occur throughout the book, and the reader is in the unique position of seeing various versions of the same incident. This is a beautiful and haunting story about the persistence of family secrets and past hurts when they are covered up rather than dealt with.

Chapter 2

The Audiophile's Audio File

Audiobooks to get you through any situation.

There are two types of people in this world—
those who like audiobooks and those who hate
them. Book purists feel the need to turn every
page by hand and want characters to have an
imagined voice. Others see audiobook-listening
as just one more way to consume books and
they appreciate the freedom that listening to a
book can provide. To me, audiobooks are magical
because they add another dimension to reading.
They provide a new level of enjoyment—or
disenchantment—because of the added tone,
tempo, and inflection that you don't get by
reading a book yourself. Characters are given
literal voices to go along with the figurative
voices the author has developed, and these
productions either involve multiple readers or,

most often, the voice of a single actor. Working in a library has shown me that audiobook readers can feel very strongly about voice actors! I know of people who will never give up on a book but will give an audiobook two paragraphs before deciding the voice actor screwed the whole thing up. Styles are continually developing, from folksy, somber, and unhurried, to wry, full cast, or musically enhanced. And nowadays audiobooks are often released at the same time hardcover versions of the book are, so you have a choice of how to consume the latest book by your favorite author. There is no denying that audiobooks are unique and convenient, because they allow for hands-free listening. You can multitask while reading, and audiobooks can be a much-needed distraction from life's mundane tasks—driving, exercising, cooking dinner, waiting in lines. Whatever your reason for listening to books on the go, here is a list of tried-and-true books with great readers.

The Accident Man (2007)
by Tom Cain, read by John Lee

••••••

Samuel Carver, a former British Marine, is an assassin who is hired to make deaths appear to be accidents. Thinking he is tasked with killing a Middle Eastern terrorist in a Paris tunnel, he is shocked to learn that he's caused the death of the world's most popular woman—Princess Diana. Determined to find out who originated the order to kill the beloved princess, Carver quickly realizes he is a loose end in the conspiracy and his ex-employers are trying to kill him. Books that fictionalize real-life incidents fascinate me, and seasoned British narrator John Lee's voice acting is perfect for this fast-paced, original thriller, the first of the Samuel Carver series.

◻ *Charlotte's Web* (1952, 1980)
by E.B. White, read by the author

• • • • • •

For as long as I can remember, it always struck me as very strange that children's books and dinner plates were both filled with farm animals. *Why would you have us read about pigs and then serve us pork chops, Mother?! And, Mother, why did you make us fear spiders when there were friendly and compassionate spiders like Charlotte around?* Needless to say, I identified so clearly with little Fern in this story, who, with the help of a spider named Charlotte, rescues a little farm pig from being killed. It wasn't until I was an adult that I listened to the fantastic audiobook. What a treat that nearly thirty years after its release it was read by the author himself with his steady, gravelly New England accent. Discover or rediscover this classic that teaches adults and children alike to open up and listen with a clear heart. And don't mind those at the gym who are staring at you as you cry for Charlotte and Fern while listening to this marvelous audio version.

◻ *A Confederacy of Dunces* (1980, 1997)
by John Kennedy Toole, read by Barrett Whitener

●●●●●●

There is nothing quite like a road trip through the South while listening to *A Confederacy of Dunces* and laughing your ass off. Listeners can easily delve into the French Quarter of New Orleans during the 1960s and the world of Ignatius J. Reilly, a giant and un-jolly sloth of a man. His colorful adventures involve his reluctant foray as a hot-dog vendor (read: eater), his prolific and egocentric feminist pen pal Myrna Minkoff, and Jones, an observant and underpaid janitor who must work or risk being dubbed a "vagran." No one besides Barrett Whitener would be quite as good at etching out Toole's rich and unique characters and their follies. You wonder how he can voice something so hilarious without cracking up.

◻ *Every Day* (2012)
by David Levithan, read by Alex McKenna

"There will always be more questions. Every answer leads to more questions. The only way to survive is to let some of them go."

• • • • • •

There aren't many authors who make it into my favorites list more than once, but David Levithan is one of them (also see *The Lover's Dictionary* in Chapter 15: YA for the Not So YA). *Every Day* is a somehow totally believable story about gender-absent A, who wakes every day in a different teenage body, in a different home, ingrained in a different life for only one day. S/he can only reach back into the memory files of the body s/he inhabits in order to get enough information to make it through the day, hopefully unnoticed. This seems to work for years until A meets Rhiannon, who becomes someone A can't leave behind. How do you convince someone you are in love with them when they see you as a different person each day? What I love most about this book is the way some of the people A inhabits make reappearances throughout the book, sort of how people in our lives reappear and make lasting impressions on us. In this audio version of the book, actress Alex McKenna does a tremendous job of drawing us into the story and providing a memorable listening experience all around.

▢ *A Free Life* (2007)
by Ha Jin, read by Jason Ma

●●●●●●

The Wu family has left China for the United States after the Tiananmen Square massacre in 1989. First settling in the Northeast and then Atlanta, Nan, the father, truly wants to be a poet but settles on running a restaurant with his wife Ping-Ping. An outsider may think that the family is well on their way down the path of the American Dream, but Nan, still heartbroken over a former girlfriend, feels that nothing could be further from the truth. Slow-paced and character-driven, this novel is a sleeper agent—quiet and understated but ultimately a powerful read that ends in a crescendo of emotions. The story is elevated by Jason Ma's flawless, matter-of-fact voice.

Ghostman (2013)
by Roger Hobbs, read by Jake Weber

*"I didn't crave attention,
I craved anonymity."*

••••••

Ghostman, a.k.a. Jack White, is a hit man living so far off the grid he can disappear right before your eyes. His jobs are so intricately planned, researched, executed, and concealed that only once did a job go awry, in Kuala Lumpur. Now hired to help cover up an Atlantic City heist gone bad, he finds that the job may be connected to enemies from his past, and is attracting the attention of a female FBI agent who may be more into Ghostman than his crimes. This dark and twisty caper, read in the deadpan and intense voice of Jake Weber, made my commute to work fly by, which is exactly what I look for in an audiobook. It might make you jumpy for a week or so, and suspicious of everyone and their intentions, like it did me.

The Good Lord Bird (2013)
by James McBride, read by Michael Boatman

"Old John Brown could work the Lord into just about any aspect of his comings and goings in life, including using the privy . . . I'd say on average he prayed about twice an hour, not counting meals."

●●●●●●

James McBride manages to take a haunting time in our history and turn it into a highly engaging satire about slavery that actually turns out to be a deep and meaningful comment on race, religion, and freedom. So many layers, just like the ones that encapsulate Little Onion, a.k.a. Henry, a freed slave thought by the fictionalized real-life abolitionist John Brown to be a girl. In the book, Onion joins Brown on the journey from the Kansas Territory to Harpers Ferry, the site of the 1859 raid that was a major catalyst for the Civil War. Book reviewer Bob Minzesheimer wrote in *USA Today* that the National Book Award judges praised McBride for having as comic and original a voice as any heard since Mark Twain. Fitting, because *The Good Lord Bird* is being referred to as an African-American take on *The Adventures of Huckleberry Finn*. And popular voice actor Michael Boatman takes the rambunctious, imaginative language and brings Onion and his story to life with a booming, smooth voice.

☐ *Motherless Brooklyn* (1999, 2001)
by Jonathan Lethem, read by Frank Muller

••••••

Giving voice to a character with Tourette's syndrome is no easy feat, but Frank Muller pulls it off brilliantly in this detective novel set in New York. Lionel Essrog is on the case when Frank Minna, the leader of a gang of orphans, is gunned down. Lionel searches for answers while dealing with physical and verbal tics, obsessive compulsions, and the type of greed and ambition that can only be found within New York crime families. Muller's mastery of the New York accent makes him highly believable as the hardscrabble detective Lionel. I was drawn to this book because I'd read an interview with the author in which he attributes the inspiration for the character with Tourette's to an essay by one of my favorite nonfiction authors, Oliver Sacks, a real-life House M.D. who writes about case studies of neurological diagnoses (see the mention of his book *The Man Who Mistook His Wife for a Hat* in the chapter called "Peculiarly True").

◻ *On Such a Full Sea* (2014)
by Chang-rae Lee, read by B.D. Wong

"We're no longer fit for any harsher brand of life, we
admit that readily, and simply imagining ourselves
existing beyond the gates is enough to induce a
swampy tingle in the underarms, a gaining chill
in the gut."

●●●●●●

In a vividly reimagined America, Fan, a fish-tank diver, leaves the safety of her labor colony in B-Mor (formerly known as Baltimore) to search for her lover, Reg, who has mysteriously disappeared. But revolution is in the air outside the gates of B-Mor, and Fan suspects Reg has been taken away to another community for medical testing. Stage and television actor B.D. Wong (think *Law & Order: SVU*) takes us on a lyrical, dystopian ride peppered with intense and action-packed scenes. I easily saw myself in Fan despite not being small, quiet, or into fish.

□ *Out Stealing Horses* (2003, 2008)
by Per Petterson, read by Richard Poe

••••••

Filled with flawed but sympathetic characters, this is the rhythmic story of Trond, a sixty-seven-year-old man who has left the city to live in a cabin in rural Norway after the death of his wife. An encounter with a neighbor stirs up memories of his boyhood, pleasant and unpleasant, particularly centered on the last summer he spent with his father when he was fifteen years old. The language and its richness stole the show for me: "One of my many horrors is to become the man with the frayed jacket and unfastened flies standing at the Co-op counter with egg on his shirt and more too because the mirror in the hall has given up the ghost. A shipwrecked man without an anchor in the world except in his own liquid thoughts where time has lost its sequence." What a huge feat for a translated book, expertly brought to life by translator Anne Born. And Richard Poe's gravelly, understated reading of the audiobook version hits all the right notes.

☐ *Prodigal Summer* (2000)
by Barbara Kingsolver, read by the author

"A breeze shook rain out of new leaves
onto their hair, but in their pursuit of eternity
they never noticed the chill."

●●●●●●

The three worlds of Deanna, a reclusive wildlife biologist, Lusa, a city girl turned farmer's widow, and feuding elderly neighbors Garnett and Nannie are intertwined during one hot summer in the mountain farms of Appalachia. There are many poignant passages in this novel. In fact, one particular passage helped a friend of mine who was grieving over the loss of a baby: "I thought I wouldn't live through it. But you do. You learn to love the place somebody leaves behind for you." That stuck with her and helped her wade her way through a dark time. Kingsolver's soothing, kind voice is perfect for this tale about the importance of balance, understanding, and continuity in nature.

Room (2010)
by Emma Donoghue, read by various readers

••••••

A story that manages to be both haunting and matter-of-fact, *Room* is told from the perspective, and in the voice, of a five-year-old boy. You may be dubious about how this goes over on audio (I was!), but it should only take a chapter or two to get used to the high squeak of Jack's voice. It also helps that there are multiple narrators for the several characters who appear in the book. Jack has spent his entire life so far in Room with Ma, Room being where Ma has been held captive for seven years by her kidnapper, Old Nick. Ma has managed to provide Jack with stability and routine but she longs to escape and needs Jack's help to do so. Despite such harrowing subject matter, I hope you are as taken with Jack as I was. I found that Jack has some really cute sayings that I appreciated more in the audio version of the book. In fact, I found myself repeating some of these sayings well after listening, my favorite being "quick quick" for "fast."

◻ *Tiny Beautiful Things:*
Advice on Love and Life from Dear Sugar (2012)
by Cheryl Strayed, read by the author

••••••

"Dear Sugar" began as Steve Almond's snarky online advice column on the popular literary website *The Rumpus* but evolved into one of the most compelling, unique, honest, relatable columns written by the one and only Cheryl Strayed. This collection contains new and previously published anonymous questions and heartfelt answers filled with empathy, sincerity, and advice that everyone can use. From a man who has a secret addiction to pain medication and is facing financial ruin to a high school girl who doesn't approve of her best friend's choice in boys to a woman who has dealt with a terribly abusive brother her entire life, I guarantee you that at least one answer or question will stop you in your tracks, cause you to listen a little harder or feel a little more, and evoke a change in your thinking. Part ad hoc memoir, part advice column, part call to live life to its fullest, this book provides the little bit of Sugar eveyone needs in their life. Check out the WBUR-produced "Dear Sugar Radio" podcast, available online (*www.wbur.org/series/dear-sugar*) in which Cheryl Strayed once again teams up with Steve Almond.

◻ *Vanished* (2009, 2010)
by Joseph Finder, read by Holter Graham

•••••••

Lauren Heller wakes in the hospital to discover that her husband, Roger, is missing—vanished—after an unknown assailant attacked the couple outside a restaurant the night before. Roger's estranged brother, Nick, is a private investigator determined to find answers, even as they point to some shady business in Roger's past. In fact, it appears that Roger has made a powerful and dangerous enemy who will do anything to stop the search in its tracks, no matter the cost. Again, my normally thirty-minute commute to work felt reduced to five minutes because of the quick step of the story and its constant twists and turns. Holter Graham's pleasant sound and attention to characters give a great voice to this fast-paced thriller.

World War Z: An Oral History of the Zombie War (2006, 2014)
by Max Brooks, read by various readers

● ● ● ● ● ●

Skip the original 2006 abridged version for the 2014 unabridged version, which features an all-star cast including Henry Rollins, Rob Reiner, Alan Alda, Simon Pegg, and Martin Scorsese among many others. *World War Z* is a documentary-flavored string of stories told from different perspectives after a virus wipes out the world as we know it and we are left with fast, chattery-teethed zombies hunting us down. With a nod to award-winning oral historian Studs Terkel, Max Brooks presents a zombie story like no other. I was surprised to learn that this is a more serious follow-up to Brooks's *The Zombie Survival Guide* (2003), a book that may or may not be set within the fictional world of *World War Z*.

Chapter 3

Daisy Dukes

Short story collections that will actually make you like short stories.

Who doesn't like short shorts? Well, lots of people. At the library, almost every week I hear people remark, "I don't normally like reading short stories." But we are missing out on some of our favorite authors' best work if we skip over their short fiction. Joyce Carol Oates, James Baldwin, John Steinbeck, Daphne du Maurier, F. Scott Fitzgerald, and Annie Proulx, among many other novelists, have all published powerful and engaging short stories.

What's so impressive about short fiction is that an author has limited him- or herself to the number of words and scenes and moments he or she can use in order to tell a captivating story. Every word truly counts. Historically, a short story didn't have a set length, but was a piece of fiction one could finish in one sitting. Interestingly, modernity may have caused a shift in that definition, since the length of time considered a "sitting" has shortened considerably—likely due to our hectic schedules and numerous life demands. Whether or not you are already a short story lover, and especially if you don't have time for an entire novel but want to experience some fantastic storytelling, check out the list that follows.

The Best of Roald Dahl (1978)
by Roald Dahl

••••••

For those familiar with Roald Dahl's magically dark children's stories, I beg you to try his stories meant for adults. This is one such collection and includes such tales as "The Man from the South," about a man who bets a young American he can't successfully light his cigarette lighter ten times in a row. If he's successful, the American wins the old man's car. If he loses, he loses a finger. This one's been adapted to film several times over the years—my favorite was a segment of *Four Rooms* by Quentin Tarantino. Dahl was inspired to write because of the stories he made up for his children as he tucked them into bed. I've always wanted to visit Great Missenden, Buckinghamshire, where Dahl lived for many years and which houses the magical Roald Dahl Museum and Story Centre.

Full Dark, No Stars (2010)
by Stephen King

● ● ● ● ● ●

Okay, so the four stories in this collection aren't exactly short stories—they're novellas—but they are oh so good. As I experienced after reading his other novella collections, *Different Seasons* (1982) and *Four Past Midnight* (1990), these stories gave me the most pleasant nightmares, particularly the one entitled "Big Driver." In this story, a female author is violently accosted and left for dead following a book-club engagement after the hosting librarian tells her to take a shortcut home. The twist at the end of the story is unbelievable. For me, there is nothing better than a new Stephen King book coming out just before an unplugged vacation at a cabin in the woods.

How to Breathe Underwater (2003)
by Julie Orringer

"I am the canker of my brother Sage's life.
He has told me so in no uncertain terms.
Tonight as we eat hamburgers in the car on the way
to our first scuba class, he can't stop talking about the
horrible fates that might befall me underwater.
This, even though he knows how scared I am after
what happened last November."

● ● ● ● ● ●

People say that your age is how you feel on the inside. If that's true, I've been eighty-three years old since I was eleven. Anyone else who has grown up this way will feel for Orringer's characters in these nine stories—young people who are flung too fast and too far into the messy corners of adulthood, to places where those around them are oblivious to their needs. Filled with memorable characters and tangible scenes, my favorite story of the collection is "The Isabel Fish," about a teen girl who recently survived drowning in an accident that killed her older brother's girlfriend, and her parents' inexplicably clueless attempt to help her confront her fear of water by signing up the siblings for scuba lessons.

Interpreter of Maladies (1999)
by Jhumpa Lahiri

●●●●●●

Preceding her novel *The Namesake*, mentioned in the chapter "American't Dream," is this multi-prize-winning collection of nine short stories centering on the Indian-American experience. In the very first story, "A Temporary Matter," a young couple reveals never-before-shared secrets to each other during the one hour of brownouts they must face for five consecutive evenings. Set against the backdrop of the moon landing, "The Third and Final Continent" is about a thirty-six-year-old man who moves to America to work at MIT and boards with the elderly Mrs. Croft while awaiting the arrival of his new wife from Calcutta. The narrator and Mrs. Croft have a strange and special bond, despite the many barriers that exist between them. Gillian Flynn, a former critic and author of *Gone Girl*, interviewed Lahiri for *Entertainment Weekly* just after she learned that she'd earned a Pulitzer for this book. During the interview, Lahiri admitted that "The Third and Final Continent" is about her own father, a university librarian. Lahiri said she was filled with anxiety over what he would think, but upon reading it, he said, "My whole life is in that story." What is most special to me is Lahiri's ability to blend the extraordinary with the ordinary and to help readers feel an intimate connection to the characters with few words.

◻ *Kissing the Witch:*
Old Tales in New Skins (1997)
by Emma Donoghue

"How was he to know what mattered to me?
Perhaps we get, not what we deserve,
but what we demand."

● ● ● ● ● ●

As long as there have been fairy tales, there have been fairy tales with a twist. This collection of thirteen tales is the best of that sort. Using the same rhythm and patterns of age-old fairy tales, Donoghue reveals characters including Cinderella and Snow White as we've never seen them before—as three-dimensional, sensual, free women who choose themselves (or even the fairy godmother) over the prince. The way these seemingly disparate stories are woven together is perfectly done. Feminist fairy tales for the win!

Knockemstiff (2008)
by Donald Ray Pollock

"My father showed me how to hurt a man one August night at the Torch Drive-in when I was seven years old. It was the only thing he was ever any good at."

••••••

The stories of complete and utter fuckeduptitude that haunt this book are gritty, dark, and, yes, even funny, albeit it's a nervous sort of laughter that will escape your lips. Intersected by time and recurring characters, the stories can be consumed alone or as a string of bleak, grim little bits. From "Hair's Fate," in which a father gives his son an unorthodox hair cut as a punishment for having sexual relations with his sister's doll, to "Bactine," which centers on the most backwoods way I've ever heard of to get high, the stories are filled with drugs, mental disorders, subversive sexual acts, and myriad methods of dying. If anyone offers you an all-expenses-paid trip to Knockemstiff, Ohio (yes, it's a real almost-ghost town near the author's hometown), run the other way.

◪ *Labyrinths:*
Selected Stories and Other Writings (1962)
by Jorge Luis Borges

••••••

From an Argentine author, librarian, dabbler in mathematics and physics, lecturer, and professor comes this collection of short fiction, essays, and parables. Perhaps the most famous of these is "Pierre Menard, Author of the *Quixote*," a mock literary review of a fictional French author who seeks to recreate Cervantes's famous work *The Ingenious Gentleman Don Quixote of La Mancha* by rewriting it, line for line. My favorite story of the collection, however, is "The Garden of Forking Paths," where readers encounter a never-ending book where at every twist and turn of the story, all possibilities are written and the branches of the story grow exponentially and into infinity. I was surprised to learn that this story isn't in fact the inspiration for the second-person Choose Your Own Adventure children's book series that was popular in the 1980s and 1990s.

⬜ *Ladies and Gentlemen* (2011)
by Adam Ross

"He imagined it was something a hummingbird must feel: an awareness of moving with great rapidity while the surrounding world remains stuck in slow motion."

••••••

And so it goes. Containing seven forty- to sixty-page stories written in matter-of-fact prose and filled with characters who could easily be your friends or neighbors, this book tugs you along for a ride through fidelity, mortality, isolation, and miscommunication between usually well-meaning folks. "When in Rome" is about a strained relationship between brothers with a violent twist, and "The Rest of It" centers on a college campus maintenance man who tells a loser professor his tales of wild adventures involving murder and drug smuggling. A theme throughout the collection is that of storytelling—or lying, as the case may be. Almost every story features a character who would make a fantastic author.

Lost in the City (1992)
by Edward P. Jones

"On an otherwise unremarkable September morning, long before I learned to be ashamed of my mother, she takes my hand and we set off down New Jersey Avenue to begin my very first day of school."

• • • • • •

Lost in the City is a collection of midcentury African-American Washington, D.C. slice-of-life stories filled with a diverse range of characters, from a loving father who wakes before his daughter to check her pigeon coop for dead birds, to the young man who finally finds his place in the work force only to be offered "severin pay" when the owner of the store decides to sell. Rich but straightforward storytelling fills this collection of fourteen stories. As the *Washington Post* journalist Neely Tucker points out, there are fourteen stories in *Lost in the City* and fourteen stories in Jones's book *All Aunt Hagar's Children*. "The first story in the first book is connected to the first story in the second book, and so on. To get the full history of the characters, one must read the first story in each book, then go to the second story in each, and so on," he writes. Isn't that wonderfully interesting? Tucker's rich interview with the author reveals Jones to be a most humble, down-to-earth, kind man, which makes me love his writing even more.

◻ *Orientation and Other Stories* (2011)
by Daniel Orozco

*"We pace our work according to the eight-hour
workday. If you have twelve hours of work in your
in-box, for example, you must compress that work
into the eight-hour day. If you have one hour of work
in your in-box, you must expand that work to fill the
eight-hour day."*

••••••

The brilliant title story of this collection begins with, well, an
orientation at your new office job. (The entire story is told in
the second-person, making "you" a specific, if universal, character.) In this office, like all offices, is a cast of colorful characters, from the woman who prophesies deaths, to the man who
sometimes uses the ladies room for no perverse (or even good)
reason, to the penguin-loving office-party planner who cries any
chance she gets. The other stories in this collection are as equally
appealing as "Orientation" because they underline the humor
of something as mundane and ordinary as the workplace.

The Outlaw Album: Stories (2011)
by Daniel Woodrell

••••••

Dropping readers right into Ozark Plateau country in the middle of America, Daniel Woodrell entrances and horrifies us with twelve short tales of off-handed murder, uncles who rape and maim, kidnapped children, arson, and other dark and gritty topics that reek of desperation and bleakness in the best way possible. Now, every time I drive through this part of the country, I think of this grim collection and wonder how many shallow graves I'm passing as I drive along the twisty roads. For more Ozark noir, also check out Woodrell's novel *Winter's Bone* (2006), featured in the chapter "My Family Is Weirder Than Yours."

◻ *Runaway: Stories* (2004)
by Alice Munro

••••••

No list of short fiction would be complete without at least one collection from Munro, the master of the genre. Within *Runaway* are eight stories about tiny, but ultimately significant, moments in the lives of women. From the weepy Carla, who is involved with a mercurial, menacing man, to Juliet, who is used to "feeling surrounded by people who wanted to drain away her attention and her time and her soul," to Robin, who discovers too late that a small misunderstanding has cost her a chance at romance, each character gains subtle insight into her thoughts, decisions, and actions. Munro's prose leaves me entranced and thoughtful, and I see traces of myself and women I know in the characters of this book.

We Wish to Inform You That Tomorrow We Will Be Killed with Our Families: Stories from Rwanda (1998)
by Philip Gourevitch

●●●●●●

In just one hundred days in 1994, 800,000 Tutsi Rwandans were massacred by the Hutu majority. Author Philip Gourevitch reached out to survivors in order to document their harrowing experiences, first in the *New Yorker*, and later within the pages of his book. The title, which came from a phrase written in a letter from Tutsi pastors to their Hutu church president, is certainly dismal, and genocide is hardly a subject one likes to recommend to another, but this book is an instructive and necessary look at how humans can treat one another. How a church leader could orchestrate and carry out the murders of his entire congregation. How an ordinary man can suddenly engage in the raping, maiming, and killing of his neighbors. How some governments sat idly by as this was going on, and how others would intervene, only to side with the killers. The author expresses it best in the opening pages: "[T]his is a book about how people imagine themselves and one another—a book about how we imagine our world." It's a sobering, eye-opening account that every human should experience and learn from.

Chapter 4

The Graphic Self

Graphic memoirs and biographies that will leave their mark.

Whether they feature panels bursting with vibrant colors or the starkness of black-and-white lines and shading, the graphics of graphic novels add a whole other dimension to a story, one that carries at least as much weight as the words on each page. The books in this chapter are all graphic memoirs or biographies, the graphic novel subgenre that happens to be my favorite. When history- or memoir-loving library patrons or friends want to dabble in the world of graphic novels, I share one or two of these titles first. From laugh-out-loud stories about the absurdity of aging like *Can't We Talk about Something*

More Pleasant? to poignant tales of coping with depression like *Hyperbole and a Half,* these are some of the best graphic biographies out there.

□ *An Age of License* (2014)
by Lucy Knisley

*"What I really love about travel is that it takes
us outside ourselves . . . it unhomes you and allows
you to see possibilities for change, growth, a new life."*

● ● ● ● ● ●

Part color, part whimsical black-and-white illustrations, this is
Knisley's travelogue about her all-expenses-paid book tour to
Europe during a time of loneliness, heartache, and uncertainty,
which of course is the best time to go on a trip by yourself! I'm
always in awe of people who travel alone, because I insist on
having a partner along to share in the adventure. Also, Knisley
has the best website (*www.lucyknisley.com*) I have ever seen, and
it contains her shop of downloadable mini books and art prints.

◻ *Blue Pills: A Positive Love Story* (2001)
by Frederik Peeters

• • • • • •

When Fred first saw Cati at a party, he was enamored by her. Years later, when they meet again, Cati has a young son and there is an immediate attraction between the two old acquaintances. They are on the cusp of a romantic involvement and things are moving along quite nicely when Cati drops the bombshell: She and her son are HIV positive. The logistics of living with HIV can be tricky, and Peeters approaches this sensitive and tender topic with compassion, humor, and grace. And I've seen first-hand at the library this book used as a springboard for discussion about HIV and how it is transmitted and treated. Rough, broad ink strokes bring this deeply personal memoir to life.

☐ *Calling Dr. Laura:*
A Graphic Memoir (2013)
by Nicole J. Georges

● ● ● ● ● ●

Growing up, Nicole Georges was told that her father died of colon cancer when she was a baby, but when she visits a palm reader at age twenty-three, she is told that her father is very much alive. Not sure what to believe, but not ready to confront her family members with whom she has a turbulent history, she keeps quiet. It isn't until years later that her sister comes clean about her father and her past. The title comes from the scene where Nicole phones a hostile Dr. Laura Schlessinger, a conservative talk radio host, for advice. This memoir is a cover-to-cover beauty with a shocking, but also unsurprising, ending.

☐ *Cancer Vixen* (2006)
by Marisa Acocella Marchetto

"Surgeries are like weddings:
They're only real when you've set a date."

••••••

Three weeks before her wedding, Marchetto, a cartoonist for *Glamour* and the *New Yorker* magazines, discovers a lump in her breast and suddenly she's in a hospital gown instead of a wedding gown. Part supercharged love story, part fashion parade, part cancer survivor story, this humorous graphic memoir covers Marchetto's battle with breast cancer. A portion of the royalties from this title goes toward cancer research, and the author also funds mammograms for uninsured women in New York City. *Cancer Vixen* is full of color and motion, just like the author.

Can't We Talk about Something More Pleasant? (2014)
by Roz Chast

••••••

Hand-lettered, in full color, and interspersed with real photos of her family and mementos, this memoir recounts the author's emotional-hilarious-enlightening experience as an only adult child coming to terms with that unavoidable something coming down the pike: her parents' aging. George and Elizabeth are sweet ("my mother even washed my father's hair for him"), close ("'Codependent?' Of course we're codependent!"), and ever practical ("maybe I'll get one pair of Quintuple Queen [pantyhose] and make three pair out of it! YES!"), but nothing can prepare these parents and their child for talking about death, money, assisted living, and the adult diaper aisle of the store—hence the title of the book. This is something we all worry about, or will one day. This special-to-my-heart book helps me feel grateful for my cadre of siblings as we begin to deal with the reality of caring for our aging parents. And it calls to mind the fact that my childhood home made it into Joel Dovev's blog-into-book *Crap at My Parents' House.* Twice.

□ *How to Understand Israel in 60 Days or Less* (2010)
by Sarah Glidden

● ● ● ● ● ●

This graphic debut is a travel memoir by Sarah Glidden, a Jewish New Yorker who travels to Israel to challenge and expand her knowledge about the Palestinian/Israeli conflict, of which she knows little. She starts out with sympathetic leanings toward the plight of the Palestinian people and critical of the Israeli government but admits she is only dimly aware of the history that brought her to that view. How brave for Glidden to honestly and openly seek out the truth about her complicated and tangled heritage, even if her mind isn't completely altered in the end. The beautiful illustrations are ink and watercolor.

◻ *Hyperbole and a Half:*
Unfortunate Situations, Flawed Coping Mechanisms,
Mayhem, and Other Things That Happened (2013)
by Allie Brosh

••••••

Anyone who has ever suffered from depression will appreciate Allie Brosh's raw, sweet, hilarious, and heart-rending tales of a life filled with solitude, frozen fear, uniqueness, and dogs. Each colorful block of pages is another tale that will deliver you up and over every little emotion you forgot you had. In a *Psychology Today* article published online, psychologist Dr. Jonathan Rottenberg writes, "I know of no better depiction of the guts of what it's like to be severely depressed: clutching your blanket, you are born into the baffling, boring, disorienting state that is depression—radically out of phase with the rest of humanity, unable to understand the concerns of other people, nor able to communicate yours to them." Brosh, the creator of the wildly popular web comic of the same name, is probably one of the funniest writers I can think of.

◻ *Isadora Duncan:*
A Graphic Biography (2008)
by Sabrina Jones

•••••

I'd somehow missed learning anything about this famous and free-spirited professional dancer until I discovered and then devoured this book. Being a self-proclaimed bisexual and very candid about her various lovers, Isadora Duncan caused quite a stir as she danced her way across the world in the early 1900s. The vivid, sparse, black-and-white drawings that adorn the pages do a great job of capturing her dance philosophy, which leaned away from rigidity and toward natural movement and inspired the next generation of her followers, dubbed "Isadorables." Her bold and inspiring life was cut short by her horrific, untimely death when her scarf was caught in the axle of the convertible in which she was riding, hurling her from the car and breaking her neck.

☐ *Maus I: A Survivor's Tale:*
My Father Bleeds History (1986)
by Art Spiegelman

••••••

This story of the Holocaust was the first graphic novel I ever consumed. This book and its sequel were born from years' worth of recorded interviews between the author and his father, a Polish Jew who survived the Holocaust, the death of a child, and the suicide of his wife. The frame narrative uses animals to represent different humans: mice for Jews, cats for Germans, and pigs for Polish non-Jews, to name a few. *Maus* became the first graphic novel to win a Pulitzer. The drawings are minimalist and deep.

◻ *Persepolis: The Story of a Childhood* (2000, 2007)
by Marjane Satrapi

••••••

In clean, sharp ink drawings, Satrapi tells the powerful story of her early childhood in Tehran during the Islamic Revolution, when the Shah is overthrown and Iran is at war with Iraq. Satrapi and those who surround her are forced to contemplate the cultural revolution and must reconcile how to simultaneously embrace religion and modernity. Smart, funny, and heartbreaking all at once, the book, originally published in four individual volumes, was combined in a single volume to coincide with the release of the film version in 2007.

Primates: The Fearless Science of Jane Goodall,
Dian Fossey, and Biruté Galdikas (2013)
by Jim Ottaviani and Maris Wicks

••••••

Many have heard of these groundbreaking scientists and researchers recruited by anthropologist Louis Leakey—Jane Goodall, who discovered much of what we know about chimpanzees; Dian Fossey, who brought awareness to the plight of the dwindling population of mountain gorillas; and Biruté Galdikas, who dedicates her life to the study of orangutans and rainforest conservation. Together, author and librarian Jim Ottaviani and illustrator Maris Wicks present a fun and informative foray into the work of these important scientists and the genesis of their passions. When I was twenty I saw Jane Goodall speak, and her gentle warmth and compassion filled the room. I sat in the front row of the auditorium and held on to her every word, and wept freely as she spoke about her work with animals and teaching humans about them. I particularly love Wicks's representation of the scientists as young girls.

◻ *The Principles of Uncertainty* (2007)
by Maira Kalman

●●●●●●

A hauntingly beautiful, existential journey through one artist's colorfully unique worldview. Kalman demands answers to such questions as *Who am I? What is anything?* and finds tiny beautiful things in her quest. I first checked out this book from the library, of course, but it soon became one of the few books I've purchased in recent years. After I did, I began carefully taking it apart, literally cutting out full pages, quotations, and illustrations. I made some poignant passages into bookmarks. I sent pages anonymously to friends I knew were struggling with mental health concerns ("My brain is exploding. Trying to make sense out of nonsense, trying to tell you everything . . . and all the while time is fleeing."). And I also sent some to friends who weren't struggling ("I am silent with gratitude. I will go and bake a honey cake and that's all."). I posted one on a city light pole next to the fancy farmers' market when no one was looking ("You cannot order a deluxe grilled cheese sandwich. There are limits to deluxe."). One or two were put up on community bulletin boards at the grocery store. I think I just wanted to share this special book in special ways—to make people who opened the envelopes or stumbled across the illustrations feel the same awe I did with the turning of each page. I hope I succeeded.

Radioactive: Marie & Pierre Curie:
A Tale of Love and Fallout (2010)
by Lauren Redniss

●●●●●●

This National Book Award finalist is a beautiful, full-color overview of the lives and love of scientists Marie and Pierre Curie. Fittingly, the couple met in a laboratory, fell in love, and embarked on a journey of romance, adventure, and scientific discovery. Marie coined the word *radioactive* and, in addition to discovering radium, discovered the chemical element polonium, which she named after her mother country of Poland. As successful as they were as scientists, the Curies were continually exposed to dangerous materials, and the couple began to sicken. The author eloquently writes: "Radioactivity had made the Curies immortal. Now it was killing them." Interspersed with rubbings, letters, collage, and colorful illustrations, this is by far one of the most beautiful graphic biographies I've ever seen or read.

❒ *The Shiniest Jewel: A Family Love Story* (2008) by Marian Henley

••••••

Marian is an unmarried, fiercely independent, forty-nine-year-old woman who is embarking on the long, frustrating, wonderful, and complicated process of adopting a baby from Russia. Anti-sentimentality and raw honesty seep through her spare cartoons as she tells friends and family her news and braces for what's next. Her mother is supportive, but her father needs a bit of time to digest the news. When he suddenly becomes ill, Marian is forced to examine their relationship and his silent and practical way of showing love.

□ *Stitches: A Memoir* (2009)
by David Small

● ● ● ● ● ●

David Small's parents waited three years to deal with the "subcutaneous cyst" growing on his neck. After the surgery, which left him with a giant scar and no voice, his parents neglected to mention to him that, oops, he actually had cancer, and oops, they know how he got it. Absolutely beautiful grayscale drawings adorn this National Book Award finalist about a pair of highly cuckoo parents, as told from the perspective of an anxious, intelligent, sweet kid who doesn't know any better until he finally does. As David learns, screaming thickens your vocal cords—this empowering story illustrates that by screaming out, sometimes we find our voice.

Chapter 5

Meta Textuals

Books about books, libraries, bookshops, and book nerds.

You've just come upon a list of books about books in a book about books. Why, yes! That's because reading books about books is a wonderfully meta way to spend time. Why read the classics when you can read about an entire bookstore or library? Don't just read; read about someone else reading! I think this way of thinking is probably why I no longer "own" books. I am a big believer in using my public library as my library. To me, books are meant to be shared or gifted, left behind on the Metro for someone to discover, or donated to the neighborhood Little Free Library. That's why I love this genre. I always wonder if the authors of books about books were sitting in a bookshop while they wrote. Does this happen in other industries? I'm sure there are songs about music and films about movies and lawsuits about lawyers. Right? Paying homage to libraries, librarians, bookshops, collectors, readers, and literature, the titles that follow celebrate books and those who love them.

☐ *How to Be a Heroine:*
Or, What I've Learned from Reading Too Much (2014)
by Samantha Ellis

"My whole life, I'd been trying to be Cathy,
when I should have been trying to be Jane."

••••••

We all have a list of books that changed us—they arrived in
our hands at just the right time, we devoured them (or savored
them), we saved them, we shared them . . . and there was a
character in each that was our friend or someone we hoped we
could become, or were. Samantha Ellis, an Iraqi-Jewish feminist
who doesn't take herself as seriously as she takes her passion
for books, is no different. Her endeavor with this book was to
revisit the titles from her younger years to see if her admira-
tion for the heroines within each held up in her adulthood. *The
Little Mermaid, Gone with the Wind, Little Women, Lace, Valley
of the Dolls,* and *A Room with a View* are just a few of the titles
she reexamined. Ellis does a fantastic job of being self-reflective
while discussing the books. Part memoir, part literary criticism,
this book contains just the right mix of well-known and obscure
titles.

◻ *If on a Winter's Night a Traveler* (1979)
by Italo Calvino

*"Watch out: it is surely a method of involving you
gradually, capturing you in the story before you realize
it—a trap."*

• • • • • •

The first several pages of this book prepare you for this book—
get comfortable, it tells you; *turn the book over in your hand*, it
says. *Go ahead and read the first several pages*, it urges. *What do
you think so far?* And then you are dropped inside a train station,
where the *real* story begins. Or does it? Every other chapter is
the start of a story—you are reading the story and then the story
cuts off and then you begin to investigate why the story cut off
and then another story begins. An examination of the writing
process and the reading process, this book feels like it was written for you, and well, it was. One of the few books written in
the second person that not only works but shines.

Mr. Penumbra's 24-Hour Bookstore (2012)
by Robin Sloan

••••••

Meet Clay Jannon, an out-of-work graphic designer who gets a part-time job at a dusty bookstore run by the mysterious Mr. Penumbra. Clay seeks help from his techie friends to decode a 500-year-old book that holds the secret to immortality. This high-tech fantasyland of Google, secret societies, and meganerds is a surreal adventure for people who love the smell of an old book but could not possibly give up their smartphones.

□   *Outwitting History:*
The Amazing Adventures of a Man Who
Rescued a Million Yiddish Books (2004)
by Aaron Lansky

••••••

In 1980, at the age of twenty-three, Aaron Lansky set out to save and preserve the world's Yiddish books. You see, scholars believed that there were fewer than 100,000 such books remaining in existence, and that did not sit well with Lansky. So he got some colleagues together and they visited aging Yiddish-speaking immigrants who owned the books; they also rescued them from attics, dumpsters, and demolition sites. This is the story of Lansky's adventure and the people he met along the way. Oh, and he also founded the National Yiddish Book Center, one of the largest Jewish cultural organizations in North America. I really admire this type of grassroots social activism, which I see practiced by people like Lansky who see a wrong and set out to right it. Saving books is an admirable thing!

◻ *The Polysyllabic Spree* (2004)
by Nick Hornby

••••••

True bibliophiles (of which you are obviously one, darling reader) will love English author Nick Hornby's month-by-month account of books purchased and books read, the titles of which rarely overlap. Each list is followed by a short essay that includes mini reviews mixed with biographical info, wit, and pep. This book will give you more ideas of what to read, what to skip, and what you probably will, but might-not-ever-and-that's-okay, read in your lifetime. This book was born from Hornby's "Stuff I've Been Reading" columns for the literary magazine *The Believer*. Also check out the other books in this series including *More Baths, Less Talking*. Hornby very clearly tells readers to "Read what you enjoy, not what bores you."

◻ *Reading Lolita in Tehran:*
A Memoir in Books (2003)
by Azar Nafisi

"[D]o not, under any circumstances, belittle a work
of fiction by trying to turn it into a carbon copy of
real life; what we search for in fiction is not so much
reality but the epiphany of truth."

●●●●●●

Librarians, teachers, and other book lovers know how liberating reading can be and how damaging and despicable censorship or information suppression is. Iranian-American teacher Dr. Azar Nafisi is no
different. In 1995 Islamic Republic of Iran, Nafisi and her students
braved raids of fundamentalist morality squads to read Western classic authors such as Jane Austen, F. Scott Fitzgerald, Henry James,
and, yes, *Lolita* author Vladimir Nabokov. Books discussed and read
freely in other parts of the world were expressly forbidden, so the
ladies met in secret in Nafisi's living room, shedding their mandatory
veils and robes to discuss the relationship between fiction and reality.
One of the most beautiful and simple takeaways of this reading journey is the fact that now, if Nafisi or any of these young women were
to revisit one of the books read during this time, they would connect it with the time spent in the living room, getting to know one
another, broadening their minds in the shadow of tyranny. Books
stay with us; they leave their marks, and, above all, they empower us
to explore ourselves and our surroundings.

The Reading Promise:
My Father and the Books We Shared (2011)
by Alice Ozma

••••••

After keeping a promise to read aloud together for one hundred consecutive nights when Alice was in elementary school, Alice and her librarian father decided to keep "The Streak" alive as long as possible. Amazingly, the duo managed to do so until Alice went away to college, and this book chronicles that reading journey. If that doesn't warm your book-loving heart, then I don't know what will. *The Reading Promise* actually made me think less about books and more about my own father and our rituals and how much I miss them. This book is an inspiration to readers and parents.

☐ *The Rise and Fall of Great Powers* (2014)
by Tom Rachman

••••••

As the title indicates, we are born, we ascend to the height of our greatness, and then we slowly decline, and bookseller and heroine Tooly Zylberberg is no different. Saddled with a mysterious past full of unanswered questions, Tooly finds that she prefers books to people. In alternating chapters that relay Tooly's story at age nine, at age nineteen, and as an adult, we learn that Tooly spent her youngest years traveling the world with a man named Paul until she made a decision at age ten that altered her course. Alluring, mysterious, and captivating, this book is filled with just the sort of characters that Tooly would like to meet.

S. (2013)
by Doug Dorst (created by J.J. Abrams)

••••••

S. is one of those books, like the Griffin and Sabine series mentioned in the chapter "Very Truly Yours," that is more book art than a novel. In it, Jennifer, a college senior, finds a well-worn book left by a stranger at the university library (*Ship of Theseus*, the final novel by a mysterious writer named V.M. Straka) that has tons of margin notes inside. Intrigued, she responds by writing back (in a different color ink) and leaves the book for its owner (who turns out to be a Straka scholar and disgraced graduate student). So you, the reader, can read just *Ship of Theseus* and its footnotes, which contain enigmatic codes and clues, or just the marginalia that is the discussion between Jennifer and Eric, or a mix of the two that just might help explain all of the mystery surrounding Straka. Whatever your approach, what happens next is an exciting, sometimes hard-to-follow but totally intriguing correspondence about the mystery of the book itself. The confusion the reader experiences is made okay by the beauty of the book and the removable photos, postcards, maps, and notes as well as the promise of catching more clues and details upon subsequent readings. This is interactive reading at its finest, almost as if the book is writing itself before your eyes.

☐ *The Shadow of the Wind* (2001)
by Carlos Ruiz Zafón

"Every time a book changes hands, every time someone runs his eyes down its pages, its spirit grows and strengthens."

••••••

Set in postwar 1945 Barcelona, *The Shadow of the Wind* is about a boy named Daniel who is captivated by a mysterious book called *The Shadow of the Wind* and its even more mysterious author, Julián Carax, who disappeared in Paris after a duel. Daniel soon learns that someone is destroying all of Carax's books, but why? And what made Daniel choose this book above all of the others in the Cemetery of Forgotten Books? Carlos Ruiz Zafón does a superb job of world-building as well as tension-building in this book about a book. A gothic magic carpet ride of delight.

The Storied Life of A.J. Fikry (2014)
by Gabrielle Zevin

●●●●●●

A.J. Fikry, a crotchety widower bookstore owner faced with dwindling sales and a dismal online presence, has a very particular list of literary dislikes, including celebrity picture books, genre mash-ups, postmortem narrators, movie tie-in editions, and "children's books, especially ones with orphans." He never imagined himself alone and angry and grieving over the unexpected death of his young wife. And then two things happen that, again, change the course of his life: A valuable book from his shop goes missing and an orphaned girl is left in his care. The baby's presence is inexplicable except for the accompanying note from the mother: "I want her to grow up to be a reader. I want her to grow up in a place with books and among people who care about those kinds of things." Residents of the quaint New England town come together to attempt to help Fikry, who, in return, plies them with books to satisfy their reading needs. This light, feel-good book about books doesn't take itself too seriously, but it's definitely an ode to reading and the magic of independent bookshops.

◻ *The Time Traveler's Wife* (2003)
   by Audrey Niffenegger

••••••

Henry, a Chicago librarian, has Chrono-Displacement Disorder, in which the sufferer is plucked in and out of moments in his life and left at a different point, completely vulnerable. Henry has known Clare, an art student, for much of his time-scattered life. Told from the perspective of both Henry and Clare, readers learn about their ups and downs, including their strange encounters (such as when Henry is thirty-six and Clare is six), and the limitations and joys of their unique relationship. Not only is the protagonist a librarian (several scenes take place in a library), but readers will also enjoy the many allusions to literary greats such as Emily Dickinson, Rainer Maria Rilke, and James Joyce. Full of laughs and heavy on foreshadowing, for which I'm a sucker, this is a time-travel romance like no other.

The Uncommon Reader (2007)
by Alan Bennett

"She was not a gentle reader and often wished authors were around so that she could take them to task."

• • • • • •

A compact novella about the (fictional) time the Queen of England happened upon a public bookmobile and discovered a love for reading, much to the chagrin of her court. You'd think that the Queen of England could spend as much time as she wanted doing anything she pleased, but her duties, christenings, dinner parties, and knightings take too much time away from her new hobby. For such a tiny book, it delivers punch after witty punch. Empathic readers can relate to Her Majesty, who is easily bored by the mundane things that take time away from reading. I am reminded of when I was young and just discovering the joy of reading. But this clever little book answers the question: what if the love of reading turns up later in life? And what if it turns up in one of the most popular figureheads in the world? As it turns out, the Queen despises the same books I do!

Chapter 6

My Family Is Weirder Than Yours

Fiction and nonfiction about
totally dysfunctional families.

Everyone thinks his or her family is zany or dysfunctional, right? Maybe you have had some dirty family laundry that came out of the dryer when you were twenty, or an uncle who hoards cats, or you yourself might deal with a disorder or two, or just have a habit of making bad life choices. But after getting a load of the nonfiction and realistic fiction titles in this chapter, from the religious fanaticism and abuse in *Jesus Land* to the lovely Edies who lived in the eventual squalor of Grey Gardens, you might think your family is completely normal (if such a thing even exists). Open up your closet and set your skeletons free before curling up with one of these little numbers.

August: Osage County (2007)
by Tracy Letts

••••••

The Weston family has gathered at their unhappy homestead in Pawhuska, Oklahoma, after sixty-nine-year-old Beverly goes missing one hot August night. His wife, Violet, her sisters and their husbands, and Beverly and Violet's adult children and their mates can't help but sling barb after barb at one another, and the dirty family secrets quickly begin to bubble up to the surface. The pill-popping, always-falling-down mother will haunt those with mother issues long after they've put this compact read down. Winner of the Pulitzer Prize for Drama, this play and its thirteen memorable characters slam into your gut and take you on a wild ride of ups and downs through family madness, rage, and secrets.

◻︎ *Chinese Cinderella:*
The True Story of an Unwanted Daughter (1999)
by Adeline Yen Mah

"Mama died giving birth to you.
If you had not been born,
Mama would still be alive."

●●●●●●

Adeline Yen Mah grew up in a viciously dysfunctional home at the hands of a sadistic stepmother, a true story reminiscent of the unjust oppression in the age-old fairy tale. Hold this book in your hands for just a moment and you'll recognize that it's Adeline Yen Mah's legacy. It's abundantly clear that she poured her heart and hope into this book. It includes a historical time-line of life in war-torn colonized China, from 1842 to 1950, as well as an invitation to unwanted children everywhere to not only persevere but to thrive despite the adversity they face. Covering her early childhood, this book follows Mah's *Falling Leaves: The True Story of an Unwanted Chinese Daughter*, which focuses more on her young adult and adult years.

Forbidden (2010)
by Tabitha Suzuma

"At what point does a fly give up trying to escape through a closed window—do its survival instincts keep it going until it is physically capable of no more, or does it eventually learn after one crash too many that there is no way out?"

● ● ● ● ● ●

Seventeen-year-old Lochan and his sixteen-year-old sister Maya have had to grow up fast. Partners in helping to raise younger siblings and supporters of one another through trials and abuse and a confusing childhood, Lochan and Maya have become so close—too close. They count down the hours at school until they can see each other alone, and even though they know their relationship is illegal, immoral, and would be incomprehensible to others, they simply can't stand to be apart. Suzuma manages to take a sensitive, taboo topic and weave a beautiful and haunting story that you know will not end well.

The Hotel New Hampshire (1981)
by John Irving

●●●●●●

Since I call my style of colorful, unusual home decor "circus chic," it occurred to me that John Irving's style of storytelling in this title could be considered "circus romp." If ever there was a darkly comedic tale about family and its inner workings and quirks, John Irving has nailed it with *The Hotel New Hampshire*. It begins with the patriarch of the family deciding that a family can survive living life in a hotel. What follows is a series of ups and downs for the bizarre family and its members. And, as in some other books on this list, there's some freaky sex stuff going on in this one—if that doesn't get you to read it, I'm not sure what will. Having read several John Irving books when I was young and then re-reading them in my thirties, I find that Irving gets better with age, and this one is no exception.

Jesus Land (2005)
by Julia Scheeres

● ● ● ● ● ●

In this memoir, Julia Scheeres shares her tremendous story about growing up with her adopted African-American brother, David, and in particular their experience at a Christian boot camp in the Dominican Republic. The abuse they suffer at the hands of their fundamentalist Christian parents and the racism they encounter in their Midwestern community will leave you gasping and enthralled. Having recently read Augusten Burroughs and *As Nature Made Him: The Boy Who Was Raised As a Girl* (2000) by John Colapinto, when I picked up *Jesus Land* I was struck by how differently children cope in order to survive adversity and how resilient and empowered these artists become as a result.

Look Me in the Eye:
My Life with Asperger's (2007)
by John Elder Robison

• • • • • •

Having been raised in a hectic and dysfunctional household, I often ruminate on the vast differences between me and my siblings, including how we see our parents and who our parents were when they raised each of us. That's why this title appealed so much to me. From the older brother of author Augusten Burroughs comes this memoir about a "social deviant" in a time before Asperger's syndrome was widely spoken about and correctly diagnosed as a mild form of autism. Be warned (or take heart) that this book is less about Asperger's and more about funny, and at times tragic, events that happened throughout his life. Read this one alongside Burroughs's *Running with Scissors* (2002) and *Magical Thinking* (2004) for an interesting look at two siblings who were raised by the same dysfunctional parents.

◻ *MemoraBEALEia:*
A Private Scrapbook About Edie Beale of Grey Gardens,
First Cousin to First Lady Jacqueline Kennedy Onassis (2008)
by Walter Newkirk

••••••

Big and Little Edie Beale of Grey Gardens are two of the most fascinating people who ever lived. Little Edie, a drop-dead-gorgeous socialite and cousin to Jacqueline Kennedy Onassis, lived her later years with her mother, Big Edie, at their East Hampton home, Grey Gardens. Despite their lavish upbringing and their famous ties, it was discovered in 1971 that the women had not only run out of money but were living in almost complete isolation, and Grey Gardens was falling apart around them. This book was specifically created for fans of the famous 1975 documentary *Grey Gardens* by brothers Albert and David Maysles and includes photos, newspaper clippings, and letters centering on Little Edie. Also be sure to check out the 2009 HBO film of the same name. The Edies are my favorite cult icons and there are far too few books about them.

☐ *The Poet Slave of Cuba:*
A Biography of Juan Francisco Manzano (2006)
by Margarita Engle

••••••

Juan Francisco Manzano (1797–1854) was born into the life
of a house slave. His first mistress treated him like a pet, forced
him to call her Mama, isolated him from other black children,
and denied him an education. His next mistress was also abusive and denied him basic necessities in the form of a power
play. This is the little-known story of Manzano, written in verse
by another poet haunted by his words. You'll want to roll these
short poems around your mouth and experience the metallic
tang of slavery and savor the earthy taste of freedom. They are
beautifully paired with the mesmerizing artwork of Sean Qualls,
expert at depicting human emotion.

Push (1996)
by Sapphire

*"Thas the alphabet. Twenty-six letters in all.
Them letters make up words. Them words everything."*

••••••

It was a struggle to decide where to list this book because the disturbing and heartbreaking title could appear in the chapter about fantastic books-into-film or audiobooks, or even the chapter on epistolary books because of the theme of journaling—but I knew, without a doubt, that this powerful book would have a place within these pages. The story of sixteen-year-old Precious Jones and the verbal, physical, and sexual abuse she suffers at the hands of her parents and on the streets of Harlem is stark. Depressing. Alarming. Brutal. Precious feels invisible except when her mother pounds her with words and fists. Then she meets the compassionate and caring teacher in her new literacy class at school and begins to form friendships with other girls in her class. In fact, the beginning of the book is rife with short, unpunctuated sentences, but by the end the syntax itself is different, the sentences longer and more complex, as Precious learns to read. She starts taking other steps to better her and her son's situation, even if it's just the beginning of what it will take to overcome seemingly insurmountable obstacles caused by a racist, classist system. I don't think it's a spoiler to say that while the ending isn't entirely hopeful, it's not entirely bleak. It is, however, realistic.

The Secret Life of the Lonely Doll:
The Search for Dare Wright (2004)
by Jean Nathan

••••••

If you've never seen Dare Wright's *The Lonely Doll* picture
books, run, don't walk, to your library and pick them up. The
Lonely Doll series, which started in 1957, tells the story of
Edith, a doll who shares her time with two teddy bears. The
books' stark black-and-white photographs, including one in
which a teddy bear is spanking Edith, are baffling and fascinating, and so is the life of the author—model and photographer
Dare Wright. Learn about how she slept in the same bed as her
mother well into adulthood, had a quasi-romantic relationship
with her brother, and may have died a virgin. The relationship
between Wright and her eccentric mother is eerily reminiscent
of the famous Beale women (see Walter Newkirk's book *MemoraBEALEia*, also listed in this chapter). From model to artist to
recluse, Wright ended life much like her doll—alone.

☐ *Sickened:*
The Memoir of a Munchausen by Proxy Childhood (2003)
by Julie Gregory

"It was usually after Mom slipped the little white pill under my tongue that my migraines got worse."

••••••

Julie Gregory grew up a sick kid—she had migraines, swollen tonsils, elusive allergies, a mysterious heart ailment. When doctors failed time and again to find a concrete diagnosis, or when they became the least bit suspicious, her mom would move on to the next doctor in the next county. It wasn't until Gregory found herself on an operating table when she was thirteen years old that she blurted out the truth to a nurse—her mother was making her sick. She'd come to realize that her mother had Munchausen syndrome by proxy and was responsible for years of repeated illnesses. The book, interspersed with medical charts, is a fascinating and terrifying inside look at what happens when your incredibly abusive mother makes you sick on purpose and medical professionals become unwitting accomplices.

Three Little Words: A Memoir (2008)
by Ashley Rhodes-Courter

"I have had more than a dozen so-called mothers in my life. Lorraine Rhodes gave birth to me. Gay Courter adopted me. Then there are the fillers."

●●●●●●

Beginning at age three when Ashley Rhodes-Courter was taken from her mother, she experienced the worst kind of foster care nightmare one could imagine in fourteen different homes. Forced to rely on the faulty child protective services system and abusive foster parents, she is kicked around from school to school and house to house, wishing and hoping to be reunited with her birth mother. This memoir was born from an essay contest that Rhodes-Courter entered in order to win scholarships for school. It's not a spoiler to say that this tremendous story has an amazing outcome: The author goes on to get a full ride to college and has graduated with honors with several degrees. She is a vocal advocate for children in the foster care system, even becoming a foster parent herself. And at the young age of twenty-six, she ran for a seat in the Florida State Senate. Rhodes-Courter demonstrates that hope matters and that young voices can be heard above all the noise.

Winter's Bone (2006)
by Daniel Woodrell

••••••

Sixteen-year-old Ree Dolly has learned some hard news: Her crystal meth–manufacturing dad has skipped bail and she, her medicated mother, and her helpless younger brothers may be turned out into the cold of winter. Unless, of course, Ree can delve into the seedy criminal world of Rathlin Valley, Missouri, to find her father—dead or alive. This is one of Woodrell's several "country noir" books set in the Ozarks, which is just a short road trip from the place I call home. That's part of the reason I was so drawn to this book and to his book of short stories, *The Outlaw Album* (2011), mentioned in the chapter "Daisy Dukes." As I read *Winter's Bone*, I imagined my shallow breaths coming out in puffs of condensation—a cold, crooked, bleak beauty of a story told with masterful prose.

Chapter 7

Peculiarly True

Crazy true stories you just can't make up.

Do you want to learn what it takes to be a crime scene cleaner? Have you ever wondered what it'd be like to live and work in a brothel? Or frequent one? Do you like real-life mysteries that lead to courtroom dramatics and end with a flourish? There is something infinitely compelling about outrageous stories that are not made up—it's why people are drawn to rubber-necking, celebrity gossip, reality shows, and juicy news articles. It's about people who care about people and lives that are not their own. What follows is a list of the best life-is-stranger-than-fiction books I love to share. Hunker down with one of the following gems and be prepared to gasp, guffaw, and wonder if you chose the right path in life.

The Art of the Steal:
Inside the Sotheby's–Christie's Auction House Scandal (2004)
by Christopher Mason

••••••

Mason—journalist, photographer, musician—tells the story of scandal and corruption by renowned auction houses that rocked the art world and resulted in the jailing of one of America's richest men in the 1990s, A. Alfred Taubman. Somehow I'd managed to miss this scandal entirely, and this book was an interesting foray into an industry I knew nothing about. What struck me the most is that the players involved in the criminal activity, namely the heads of Christie's and Sotheby's, had laid the groundwork for cheating their clients out of millions of dollars many years before. The result of the scandal included resignations, arrests, time served, and over $512 million paid out in civil suits.

◻ *Beyond Belief:*
The Secret Lives of Women in Extreme Religions (2013)
by Susan Tive and Cami Ostman

••••••

Despite living my life without it, religion fascinates me. So much so that I almost accidentally minored in religious studies as an undergraduate because I kept taking class after class, wanting to understand why and what people believe. And after college, I devoured books on the subject, like this one. Discover the captivating and oftentimes heart-wrenching true stories about women who experienced extreme religions, from a deconverted born-again (dead-again?) Christian to a woman who spent years in Orthodox Judaism to a woman born to fundamentalist Pakistani Muslim parents. The subjects explain what they believed, how others perceived them, why they stayed, and what they miss about the communities they eventually left. Near the end of the book are bios of the contributors, many of whom are writers (one of whom is Julia Scheeres, whose book *Jesus Land* appears in the chapter titled "My Family Is Weirder Than Yours").

◻ *Brothel:*
Mustang Ranch and Its Women (2001)
by Alexa Albert

• • • • • •

What began as a public health survey by a Harvard Medical School student evolved into a six-year study of the famous Mustang Ranch, a legally operated house of prostitution in Nevada. After a troubled history involving tax fraud, racketeering, and even murder, along with several changes in ownership (but it was never operated by the U.S. government, as urban legend suggests) and a move, Mustang Ranch is still operating in Sparks, Nevada. Today they provide public tours and their website reveals a forum for reviews—by customers and the Mustang women.

☐ *Don't Let's Go to the Dogs Tonight:*
An African Childhood (2001)
by Alexandra Fuller

••••••

Alexandra "Bobo" Fuller grew up a white minority in Zimbabwe (then Rhodesia), where everyone learned how to use a gun by age five, racism and mistrust between the black majority and the white minority were rampant, and terrs (terrorists) and scorps (scorpions) were so prevalent that they had nicknames. Presenting her story in "this is how it was" fashion, Fuller doesn't sugarcoat anything, nor does she comment on her unusual upbringing. It surprised me, actually. Its absence makes for a very unique viewpoint and allows space for the reader to examine his or her own life and views on race, equality, and social justice.

◻ *The Executioner's Song* (1979)
by Norman Mailer

● ● ● ● ● ●

Behold this giant tome, this true-life novel in a similar vein as Truman Capote's *In Cold Blood* (1966). When Gary Gilmore was released from prison at the age of thirty-six he was ready to find a job and settle down as a free man. However, his plan for a simple life without crime quickly went awry. In case you have never read the book and don't know what happened to Gilmore, I'm not going to supply you with any of the answers here, because I did not have that knowledge going into this book in high school. I read it without any preconceived notions about what happens to this internationally infamous criminal who inspired the song by the Adverts, "Gary Gilmore's Eyes." In his essay "Mailer's Sad Comedy: *The Executioner's Song*," biographer Robert Merrill quotes Mailer as saying, "[Gilmore] appealed to me because he embodied many of the themes I've been living with all my life long." This quotation is what made me want to read the book and then learn all that I could about Norman Mailer, a complicated man. Mailer won his second Pulitzer Prize for this book.

The Man Who Mistook His Wife for a Hat
and Other Clinical Tales (1985)
by Oliver Sacks

••••••

The most engaging book about medical case studies out there! Dr. Oliver Sacks, a British-American neurologist, tells about patients struggling to live with severe disorders. The title essay is about a man who suffers from visual agnosia, a condition that makes it impossible to distinguish between certain visually presented objects. Like hats and wives. Other essays feature stories about autistic savants, people who feel disembodied because of a condition called proprioception, and a twenty-two-year-old man who wakes after a night of drug use to find that he has a dramatically heightened sense of smell—the latter being most interesting to me because Sacks later admits that he is the subject in this case. This book inspired an opera by the same name by Michael Nyman.

◻ *Mop Men:*
Inside the World of Crime Scene Cleaners (2004)
by Alan Emmins

••••••

While pitching stories to his editor at a men's lifestyle magazine, author and journalist Alan Emmins realized with discomfort and curiosity that stories about people dying grab attention. That in the world of entertainment, death sells. If he wanted to sell articles and write books, he'd have to find a deadlier subject than what he was used to writing about. Enter Neal Smither, the subject of *Mop Men*. The idea for his business, Crime Scene Cleaners, Inc., came from watching the film *Pulp Fiction*. After the CSI team leaves the scene of a murder, accident, or suicide, Smither and his team are hired to go in and ensure that not a speck of blood or gore is left behind for anyone else to deal with. A court case that takes place throughout the course of the book is enthralling and leaves the reader hoping for justice. Emmins takes a morbid subject and deals with it compassionately and with sensitivity for the victims and the people they leave behind.

◻ *The Rape of Nanking:*
The Forgotten Holocaust of World War II (1997)
by Iris Chang

••••••

There are many things I should've learned about before attending college, but at the top of the list are: the Tulsa Race Riot of 1921, the World War I–era Armenian genocide, and the topic of this book. Extensively researched and highly readable, this is an account of the Japanese massacre of more than 300,000 Chinese residents in (what is now) Nanjing during 1937–38. Told from three unique perspectives (the victims, the oppressors, and the saviors), this book inspired me to read all that I could about the massacre. Also compelling is the story of the young author's 2004 suicide and the questions and conspiracy theories it raised. For further reading, look for the harder-to-find book *The Rape of Nanking: An Undeniable History in Photographs* (1997) by James Yin and Shi Young.

☐ *Stiff: The Curious Lives of Human Cadavers* (2003)
by Mary Roach

*"Being dead is absurd. It's the silliest situation
you'll find yourself in. Your limbs are floppy and
uncooperative. Your mouth hangs open. Being dead is
unsightly and stinky and embarrassing, and there's not
a damn thing to be done about it."*

••••••

Except write about it! And write about it well, as Mary Roach
certainly has. From the mechanics of human decay to the likeli-
hood of a human head transplant, Mary Roach has only interesting but true, funny but respectful things to say about death.
And don't skip her footnotes, which is where most of the humor
happens. Roach's other popular science books (on the themes
of sex, space, food, and the afterlife) are also not to be missed.

The Swerve: How the World Became Modern (2011)
by Stephen Greenblatt

●●●●●●

History buffs unite! Two thousand years ago, a Roman named Lucretius wrote a philosophical epic poem called *On the Nature of Things*, the Epicurean subjects of which (religion, sex, the idea that life is made up of atoms that randomly swerve, creating serendipitous collisions and acts of free will) are still highly debated today. Lost to history for one thousand years after it was penned, it was later found in a monastery by a book hunter in 1417. All of this is interesting, but even more so is the fact that the rediscovery of the poem paved the road to modernity as we know it. *The Swerve* won the 2012 Pulitzer Prize for General Nonfiction as well as the 2011 National Book Award for Nonfiction.

◻ *They Marched Into Sunlight:*
War and Peace, Vietnam and America, October 1967 (2003)
by David Maraniss

••••••

Like the best arguments, the best historical narratives are approached from multiple angles, and Maraniss does not let us down. Told through the events of a few days at the height of the Vietnam War in October 1967 and based on primary documents and interviews, this book introduces us to American and Viet Cong soldiers, professors, a future vice president, antiwar students back home, and those in charge in Washington, D.C. This amazingly researched and well-indexed book was made into an award-winning PBS documentary film titled *Two Days in October*, and Tom Hanks and Gary Goetzman own the rights to a feature film version. So much has been written about the Vietnam War, but this is the first nonfiction piece that held and heightened my interest in the topic.

☐ *The Warmth of Other Suns:*
The Epic Story of America's Great Migration (2010)
by Isabel Wilkerson

●●●●●●

From 1915 to 1970, millions of black Americans fled the South in search of a better life in the North or West. Wilkerson frames the telling of this historical migration by focusing on three individuals: Ida Mae Gladney, a sharecropper who left Mississippi for Chicago in 1937; George Starling, a civil rights activist who fled Florida for Harlem in 1945; and Robert Foster, who left Louisiana in 1953 and who later became personal physician to Ray Charles. The stories of these three individuals are interwoven with catalysts and hopes for the moves and the challenges African Americans faced on the journey and upon arrival at their destination in the warmth of another sun. Wilkerson is the first black woman to win a Pulitzer in journalism.

The Wild Trees:
A Story of Passion and Daring (2007)
by Richard Preston

●●●●●●

This is a fantastic story of the curiosity, adventure, and daring that compel a group of young explorers to climb the tallest trees in the world—the coastal redwoods of Northern California. Their research and determination paid off, and not only did they climb the trees, but they also discovered the previously unknown ecosystems that exist in the tree canopies. Lichen and berries and small animals, never thought to have lived there, were observed and researched by Marie Antoine and Steve Sillett. Even the author tried his hand at redwood climbing! I learned more about tree-climbing organizations, fire caves, and what it takes to make love in a hammock hundreds of feet from the ground than I ever thought possible. It reads like an adventure novel and makes me want to go climb a (short and manageable) tree. If this intrigues you, check out Preston's arguably more famous book *The Hot Zone: The Terrifying True Story of the Origins of the Ebola Virus* (1994), a nonfiction page-turner like no other.

Chapter 8

Reel Good Books

Books-into-movies that won't make you gag.

Nothing cracks me up more than walking out of a movie based on a book and hearing audience members tell it like it is: "It was NOTHING like the book. UGH." or "You liked it?! But did you READ the book?" I especially love it when they humblebrag, "It's hard to remember how the book ended; it's been SO LONG since I read it." As for me, I absolutely love it when a beloved book is made into a film. To see how another artist adapts it and makes it his or her own to release into the wild is exciting. And what a challenge it is to take words on a page and change them into sights and sounds to be devoured in ninety minutes or so. From *The Girl with the Dragon*

Tattoo to *True Grit* to *To Kill a Mockingbird*, what follows is a list of films that will actually spur a debate between you and your book-clubber friends about whether a particular film or book was better. Read the book first or see the movie first; it really doesn't matter. The important thing is that you are reading and discussing books and their adaptations.

The Bad Seed (1954)
by William March

••••••

I loved the wicked, pigtailed main character of this book so much that I named a kitten Rhoda Penmark after her, and boy, was that cat naughty! Later a play and then a film, this classic is about an eight-year-old girl who seems perfect in every way, but oh wouldn't you know it, she's a serial killer. Adults don't suspect her, but the kids in the story are smart enough to keep their distance. Patty McCormack, the actress who plays little Rhoda Penmark, was nominated for an Academy Award for Best Supporting Actress.

The Children of Men (1992)
by P.D. James

●●●●●●

In dystopian England in the year 2021, humankind is infertile and the last child was born twenty-five years earlier. People are listlessly killing time, waiting to go extinct. Told through a former teacher's diary entries (for Theo has no one left to teach!) and through narration, the story waxes philosophical on humanity and our mortality. When it is discovered that a woman is pregnant, Theo finds himself inextricably involved in protecting her. My favorite passage is this one, obviously: "The children's books have been systematically removed from our libraries. Only on tape and records do we now hear the voices of children, only on film or on television programmes do we see the bright, moving images of the young. Some find them unbearable to watch but most feed on them as they might a drug." The film adaptation was created in 2006, fourteen years after the publication of the book.

Chocolat (1999)
by Joanne Harris

••••••

Something deliciously bewitching happens to the sleepy French village of Lansquenet when Vianne Rocher and her daughter, Anouk, arrive to open a confectioner's shop at the beginning of Lent. Vianne's sweets seem to cure what ails the town's residents, but is the indulgence a curse or a blessing, a pleasure or sin? Soon it ceases to matter to the town's residents, who cannot get enough pain au chocolat, rose creams, and bonbons, much to the dismay of Father Francis Reynaud. I love this story for calling Lansquenet's rigid sense of morality into question. The tones of film and book are different but equally satisfying. Be sure to cozy up to the fire with some rich hot chocolate as you read this one, and then enjoy the film adaptation starring Juliette Binoche, Judi Dench, and Johnny Depp.

◻ *The Cider House Rules* (1985)
by John Irving

• • • • • •

Irving's sixth published novel was adapted into an award-winning 1999 film directed by one of my favorites, Lasse Hallström. The story focuses on Homer, a young man who has grown up in a country orphanage lovingly run by a doctor who performs illicit abortions for women in need. Homer becomes trained in medicine, albeit he's unlicensed, but then goes to work on an apple orchard for a change of scenery. It's there that he learns more about the world than ever before—whether or not he's ready. The all-star cast featuring Tobey Maguire, Charlize Theron, Michael Caine, and Paul Rudd does a terrific job with the film version of this famous story about compassion, fidelity, and honesty in the face of conflict.

The Girl with the Dragon Tattoo (2005)
by Stieg Larsson

●●●●●●

One of the best things I have ever been gifted with was one of those ubiquitous silicone wristbands that reads, "What Would Lisbeth Do?" after the main female badass Lisbeth Salander in this series of books and films. Mikael Blomkvist, a journalist who is down on his luck, is hired to research and solve an eccentric family's mystery and hires Lisbeth, a genius hacker, to help. Soon they are both swept into a dangerous situation as they step on toes in order to get closer and closer to solving the mystery. I love that Lisbeth isn't femmed up or dumbed down in either the American or Swedish film—she is just as intelligent and tough and misunderstood as she is in the books. This one is not for the faint of heart, which is also a big draw for me.

The Godfather (1969)
by Mario Puzo

••••••

Mafia fiction at its finest! As is Sicilian tradition, Don Vito Corleone, a brutal but fair man, receives special requests on the day of his daughter's lavish wedding, including one from a man seeking vengeance against his daughter's attackers. As FBI agents stake out the wedding, something is brewing and it heavily involves one of the most feared characters in literature and film: Luca Brasi. Puzo not only wrote the book and its sequels, but also had a hand in the screenplay of the legendary 1972 film starring Marlon Brando, James Caan, Al Pacino, and Robert Duvall under the impressive direction of Francis Ford Coppola.

◻ *High Fidelity* (1995)
by Nick Hornby

● ● ● ● ● ●

Maybe it's because the main character, Rob, loves making lists and overexamining stuff. Or maybe it's because John Cusack's portrayal of him reminds me of my goofy, but complicated, older brother Jayson. Whatever the combination of reasons, this book and its movie adaptation have a very special place in my heart. Thirty-year-old Rob may be an expert about records and music, but he is most definitely not an expert on manhood and relationships. This is not your run-of-the-mill dude lit—we all can learn from Rob's insecure internalizing, fretting over how much to reveal of ourselves to those we love, and the inclination to romanticize shitty past relationships.

◻︎ *Miss Pettigrew Lives for a Day* (1938)
by Winifred Watson

••••••

When I was in graduate school, I had nary a moment for pleasure reading—getting my library science degree was all business
and a year-round affair. This is the one book I read for pleasure
during that time and I couldn't have chosen a more entertaining
book. In it, Miss Pettigrew, a prim and proper governess, arrives
at the wrong address for an interview. Instead of a house full of
English children, she encounters the glamorous, risqué night-
club singer Delysia LaFosse, who becomes her new employer.
Both of the women's lives are forever changed over the course
of the novel—a single day. How lucky for me that just one year
after my graduating, seventy years after its publication date, the
film adaptation came to be, starring Amy Adams and one of my
favorite actresses, Frances McDormand, who plays the beloved
Miss Pettigrew.

The Prize Winner of Defiance, Ohio: How My Mother Raised 10 Kids on 25 Words or Less (2001)
by Terry Ryan

••••••

Evelyn Ryan, mother of ten and wife to an alcoholic, violent man, won hundreds of jingle-writing contests in the 1950s and '60s out of sheer necessity and ingenuity. She won money, refrigerators, bicycles, and many household items her adult children sorted after her death—a task that was the catalyst for the siblings to share stories and that led to the writing of this memoir. In the boxes of items were copies of Evelyn's jingles, which are sprinkled throughout the loving memoir. This unique remembrance was brought to the big screen in 2005, and stars Julianne Moore and Woody Harrelson. Sadly, just a few years after the film's release, Terry Ryan died of lung cancer at age sixty. The *San Francisco Chronicle* article about her passing reads, "When she appeared at a local screening of the film in 2005, cancer was clearly sapping her energy. Still, Ryan told a reporter, 'You have to always, always look at the positive side and don't get lost in the negative.' It is an attitude that Evelyn Ryan passed along like a legacy."

Requiem for a Dream (1978)
by Hubert Selby Jr.

••••••

Sarah Goldfarb wants nothing more than to lose weight and appear on a game show. Her son Harry and his girlfriend Marion and best friend Tyrone hatch a plan to become insta-rich by acquiring a pound of uncut heroin, but things get worse and worse for all involved. A powerfully honest look at four lost souls dependent on drugs and the illusion of hope. Let yourself spiral along the slow descent of each of the characters and then prepare to be terrified by the film adaptation. This startling book could just as easily have been placed in the chapter titled "American't Dream," but the 2000 film directed by Darren Aronofsky was oh so good, I would be remiss not to include it here.

The Road (2006)
by Cormac McCarthy

••••••

Don't beat me, but this is one of just a few books that I loved slightly less than the film adaption, directed by John Hillcoat and starring Viggo Mortensen and Charlize Theron, among other biggies. *The Road* is about a man and his young son trying to make it in a bleak, gray, post-apocalyptic world where civilization, time, animals, and vegetation no longer exist. An unexplained event a few years before caused this new landscape where the biggest threats are hunger and the cannibals who roam the land. Also check out McCarthy's *Outer Dark*, which is described in the chapter "Southern Discomfort."

☐ *The Shipping News* (1993)
by Annie Proulx

●●●●●●

Reading this novel, set in the freezing and stark milieu of New-foundland, will send chills over your skin and might make you believe you can see the condensation of your breath, and watching the film has the same effect. Quoyle (pronounced "coil") takes his two daughters and moves to his ancestral home of Newfoundland after he is emotionally beaten to a pulp by his two-timing wife. This story is a bleak but mystical trudge through life and loss and learning to live with what you have. Proulx is hypnotic with words and a master at character-naming (besides Quoyle, see Petal, Bunny, and Sunshine). The 2001 film is another favorite of mine by Lasse Hallström, starring Kevin Spacey.

To Kill a Mockingbird (1960)
by Harper Lee

••••••

Atticus Finch was my biggest childhood crush. There, I said it. After first reading this masterpiece in roughly eighth grade, I was captivated by this character—a man who was kind to children, animals, and housekeepers, a man who fought for social justice, a man who would nickname his daughter Scout! Yes, I loved him very much, and when I got around to watching the film version starring Gregory Peck, I loved him even more. Side note: when I was in library school at the University of Alabama in 2006, I became aware that Harper Lee herself was in the library somewhere. I tried to play it cool but simply gawped at her from my place at the catalog computer. It's the closest I've gotten to swooning due to a celebrity.

True Grit (1968)
by Charles Portis

••••••

The only western that appears in *Check These Out*, *True Grit* features one of my favorite female characters: Mattie Ross. Mattie is just fourteen when her father is robbed and killed in Arkansas by Tom Chaney, a "short man with cruel features." In order to avenge his death, she convinces Rooster Cogburn, the meanest U.S. Marshal around, and a Texas Ranger named LaBoeuf to accompany her on a journey to find Chaney. Adventure and tomfoolery ensue as the trio learns they are stronger together than apart. I highly recommend both of the feature films made after this book. The 1969 version, starring John Wayne as Rooster, earned Wayne an Academy Award, and the 2010 Coen brothers film, starring Jeff Bridges, earned ten Academy Award nominations.

Chapter 9

Southern Discomfort

Spooky reads set in the American South.

Let's face it: Books are just spookier when they are set in the American South. Maybe it's the tendrils of Spanish moss hanging from the old live oak trees, the South's deep and disturbing Civil War and civil rights history that permeates the fabric of the region, that specific shade of "haint blue" paint on porches thought to keep the ghosts away, the hoodoo of the Mississippi Delta, the misty swirl of Florida swampland, or the beautiful ballast stone streets that threaten to twist an ankle. Or maybe it's the slow way of talking and living and changing. Whatever the combination, setting is a major player in the books listed in this chapter. As you open each of these books, you may feel the hot breath of the Deep South. And it will chill you to the bone.

by Toni Morrison

"Not a house in the country ain't packed to
its rafters with some dead Negro's grief.
We lucky this ghost is a baby."

••••••

Sethe was born a slave. She managed a harrowing escape to Ohio but is haunted by her memories of Sweet Home—the plantation she was forced to work on—and the ghost of her baby, nameless except for the single word she could afford to have etched onto her tombstone: Beloved. Sethe lives with her daughter Denver and her mother-in-law Baby Suggs. Suddenly, a mysterious new-comer arrives and calls herself "Beloved." Beloved throws things out of balance and soon encapsulates the scars and terror that come from a history of people enslaving people. Profoundly lyri-cal, this book contains my favorite last two pages in all of litera-ture, including this passage: "By and by all trace is gone . . . [t]he rest is weather. Not the breath of the disremembered and unac-counted for, but wind in the eaves, or spring ice thawing too quickly. Just weather. Certainly no clamor for a kiss." Although this isn't listed in the chapter "Reel Good Books," I was fascinated to learn about the character treatment Oprah Winfrey gave Sethe before and during the filming of the movie version, including being blindfolded and left in the woods in order to get an inkling of what it had been like for a runaway slave.

The Bottoms (2000)
by Joe R. Lansdale

••••••

I'm a sucker for serial killers, mysteries, boogeymen, and coming-of-age stories, and this one contains all four with masterful storytelling. Harry Crane, an eighty-something nursing home resident, tells us about when he was eleven years old in Depression-era East Texas, where a brutal serial killer was on the loose. In fact, he and his sister Thomasina found the body of the first victim in the woods while discussing the legendary boogey creature, the Goat Man. The investigation of the crimes quickly begins to peel back the thin layers of rampant racism and hatred just beneath the surface of the town.

The Cutting Season (2012)
by Attica Locke

● ● ● ● ● ●

Caren, manager of the historic Louisiana plantation turned tourist site Belle Vie, should have known that "one day it would spit out what it no longer had use for, the secrets it would no longer keep." This certainly seems true when the body of a woman, her throat cut, is found on her watch at the fence line between the plantation and the fields of sugarcane now owned by an ambitious corporation. When Caren learns about the long-ago disappearance of a former slave, she wonders if the deaths are somehow tied across time. The Cutting Season is a multifaceted mystery set against the perfect backdrop of an eerie Southern tourist destination replete with restored slave quarters and Civil War reenactments.

A Grown-Up Kind of Pretty (2012)
by Joshilyn Jackson

••••••

The covers of Jackson's books make them seem like sweet Southern belle romances, but don't be fooled—most are dark and twisty tales filled with cuckoo characters who suck you in, chew you up, and spit you out onto the hot Southern asphalt. *A Grown-Up Kind of Pretty* is the tale of three generations of women from the same Alabama family—Big, forty-five, mother of Liza, thirty, mother of Mosey, fifteen. Family lore says that "Every fifteen years God flicks at us with one careless finger and we spin helplessly off into the darkness." And it hits: Liza has a stroke and a family mystery involving an unearthed backyard grave begins to unfold. Twists and turns galore! Also listen to her audiobooks, which Jackson, an actress, narrates.

Hell at the Breech (2003)
by Tom Franklin

"[E]ver time you do something, no matter what it is,
if it's whacking a croquet ball or catching a fish, ever
time you do a thing, the next time it's a mite easier.
And finally you get to be good at catching fish, or
playing croquet, or even killing. You get to where you
can do it without thinking."

• • • • • •

This novel is loosely based on the horrific incidents known as the Mitcham War, which occurred mere miles from the author's childhood home in rural Alabama. In the book, in 1897, a group of white cotton farmers formed a secret society called Hell-at-the-Breech in order to avenge the murder of a public figure. What follows is a mix of fact and fiction based on the nearly forgotten gang that terrorized the town, causing a year-long campaign ending in violence and murder.

▢ *Midnight in the Garden of Good and Evil* (1994)
by John Berendt

••••••

This book inspired me to move to the coastal city of Savannah, Georgia, for a year before I started graduate school. It's every bit as enchanting and bewitching as Berendt portrays. Berendt, a magazine columnist, discovered the beautiful Southern city for himself when he and some friends realized that plane tickets to other cities could be purchased for about the same amount of money as a night out in New York City. So he begins to explore different cities and happens upon Savannah in the midst of the compelling trial of antiques dealer Jim Williams for the murder of his live-in assistant and maybe lover, Danny Hansford. This easy-to-digest true story is about the oddball characters Berendt meets while visiting and chronicling the trial. When I lived there, I heard many rumblings from long-time residents about how the book, which bolstered tourism, was more of a curse than a blessing, but I still encourage everyone I know to visit at least once. Such a beautiful, haunted place!

Mudbound (2008)
by Hillary Jordan

● ● ● ● ● ●

The paradox of black soldiers who came home to racial bigotry and segregation after fighting in World War II is explored in this novel by Hillary Jordan. How could we expect a soldier to fight for justice and then come home to injustice? Perhaps that's why *Mudbound* so captivated me. Laura is uneasy on her husband Henry's Mississippi Delta farm. After the war ends, her brother-in-law, Jamie McAllan, and a black veteran named Ronsel Jackson, the son of the sharecroppers on McAllans' land, come to work on the farm and become fast friends, much to the chagrin of the townsfolk. Laura is the first to foreshadow the complex and haunting story of what happens in 1946 between the McAllans and the Jacksons: "The truth isn't so simple. Death may be inevitable, but love is not. Love, you have to choose." Told in alternating chapters, *Mudbound* is a winner of the Bellwether Prize for fiction, awarded to a first literary novel that addresses issues of social justice.

Outer Dark (1968)
by Cormac McCarthy

••••••

In short, straightforward sentences and chapters, this dark and brooding novel is akin to McCarthy's *The Road* in that it's a bleak journey made on foot, but *Outer Dark* takes place long ago (before there were cars), somewhere in gritty Appalachia. After bearing her brother Culla's baby, Rinthy learns that their baby did not in fact die as Culla would have her believe. Rinthy sets off alone to find the baby, who has since been discovered by a traveling tinker. Culla leaves on his own journey to find work and salvation from his sins. There's also a dangerous gang on the loose. This book probably has the most shocking, horrific ending of any book I've ever read. And no one has ever accused me of having a faint heart.

A Quiet Belief in Angels (2007)
by R.J. Ellory

••••••

Melodic prose fills this crime novel/family saga that centers on Joseph Vaughan as events from his childhood haunt him throughout his life from age twelve to sixty. He is determined to find the serial murderer of the young girls in his hometown of Augusta Falls, Georgia. Finally, years later, a neighbor is found hanged and surrounded by the murder victims' possessions. And the killings stop. Joseph goes on with life even as his mother suffers a breakdown and he is later arrested and falsely imprisoned for a decade. When the killings begin again, Joseph learns a startling truth that brings him back into the center of the murders. Illuminating and frightening, this book gave me nightmares the night after I closed the cover. That's always a sign of a good book in my eyes.

Serena (2008)
by Ron Rash

••••••

Serena Pemberton is strong, cunning, and unrelentingly vicious with anyone who threatens her intense life with her new husband in the logging country of Depression-era North Carolina. She's tough and can log with the best men. And she hunts rattlesnakes. When she learns that she can't bear children of her own, she sets out to destroy the illegitimate child her husband sired without her. Even though she has been called one of the most ruthless female characters in literature, I find her unapologetic badassery completely appealing. "When a crew foreman asked Doctor Cheney what Mrs. Pemberton would want the snakes for, the physician replied that she milked the fangs and coated her tongue with the poison." Yep.

A Walk on the Wild Side (1956)
by Nelson Algren

"Never play cards with a man called Doc.
Never eat at a place called Mom's.
Never sleep with a woman whose troubles
are worse than your own."

••••••

This American classic that has fallen through the cracks contains every downtrodden character you can picture—thieves, rapists, prostitutes, pimps, addicts, nomads, and the lonesome. Dove Linkhorn is an illiterate drifter set on wandering the Southern countryside after a failed love affair. He bounces from town to town and woman to woman leaving nothing but misery in his wake. The worst of his debauchery culminates in New Orleans and involves a condom factory, a brothel, and a fight to the finish. Some of the most despicable characters in literature can be found within this one book.

◻︎ *Wise Blood* (1952)
by Flannery O'Connor

••••••

This novel, O'Connor's first, centers on Hazel Motes, a veteran who returns from World War II to find that his family home in Tennessee has been abandoned. A devoted atheist, he buys a suit and hat and decides to do some anti-religious street preaching. Motes meets a cast of nefarious characters along the way, including a prostitute, a zookeeper, a blind preacher and his nymphomaniac daughter, and a mummified dwarf. The most hilarious scene comes when eventually a con man decides to parody Motes's anti-religious movement by forming his own ministry, called "The Holy Church of Christ Without Christ," which makes him lots of money and, of course, angers Motes to no end. O'Connor's only other novel, *The Violent Bear It Away* (1960), also deals with religion.

Chapter 10

Tales of Woe, Tales of Whoa

*Tearjerkers that will make you
snot all over the place.*

Sometimes you're just in the mood for a heartbreaker. Maybe you've had a bad day or are going through a breakup or are incredibly happy and want to remind yourself just how lucky you are. Like tearjerker movies and sad songs, there is a time and place for woeful books, although some, such as many in the following list, might sneak up on you. The best sad books maintain a delicate balance between humor and despair to deliver the reader over the peaks and through the valleys of emotion, so that we feel the highs along with the lows. And isn't that how life works? When tragedy strikes, life doesn't stand still. Whatever your reason for wanting to wallow in the depths of despair for a few hundred pages, these books are guaranteed to make you weep, bawl, and snot all over your favorite shirt.

The Art of Racing in the Rain (2008)
by Garth Stein

*"These are things that only dogs and women understand
because we tap into the pain directly, we connect
to pain directly from its source, and so it is at once
brilliant and brutal and clear, like white-hot metal
spraying out of a fire hose, we can appreciate the
aesthetic while taking the worst of it straight in the face.
Men, on the other hand, are all filters and deflectors
and timed release. For men, it's like athlete's foot: spray
the special spray on it, they say, and it goes away."*

••••••

On the eve of the narrator's death, he's reflecting on love, family, loyalty, and life. Did I mention that the narrator is a dog obsessed with opposable thumbs? I always wonder what my darling cats would say about our family—does Buffy have loyal thoughts of me or is it all about the food? Is Fez truly a cantankerous grandpa or is he just contemplative? I don't think I'm any closer to knowing having read *The Art of Racing in the Rain* (probably for the best), but it's fun to think about.

Bee Season (2000)
by Myla Goldberg

••••••

Picking this book up and thinking "Oh, here's a nice little book about spelling bees, la-di-da!" would be a mistake. Eliza Naumann, a mediocre student who longs for acceptance, surprises everyone in her overachieving family by winning a spelling bee that catapults her to a national competition. Her Jewish mystic father finally takes her under his wing, usually a place reserved for her brother Aaron, and the already tepid family dynamic is threatened. Soon, Eliza is studying spelling words, her father is obsessing over Kabbalah, Aaron is exploring other religions, and Eliza's mother's deep, dark secret is exposed. *Bee Season* is an intimate portrait of a family unraveled.

⬜ *Cane River* (2001)
by Lalita Tademy

• • • • • •

Cane River is a fictionalized but highly researched saga of Tademy's maternal descendants in Creole Louisiana, told from the perspective of four women from the same family. The stories span from matriarch Elisabeth, who was brought to Cane River as a slave from Virginia in 1820, to her great-granddaughter Emily, the last of the family born into slavery. Emily, Lalita Tademy's great-grandmother, died in 1936 with $1,300 in cash hidden beneath her mattress. Especially captivating is the string of interracial marriages, some forced and some chosen, that dot the history of Tademy's family, and the implications of light versus dark skin in the family and how skin color is viewed over time. Also check out Tademy's book *Red River* (2007), which is about her father's side of the family.

The Chronology of Water (2011)
by Lidia Yuknavitch

*"Little tragedies are difficult to keep straight.
They swell and dive in and out between great
sinkholes of the brain."*

••••••

The Chronology of Water is a slow, melodic memoir that is broken into several sections. In "Holding Breath," Yuknavitch describes suffering through a still birth and lying to strangers, saying that her child is alive and well: "In day care she is already drawing pictures!" The section called "The Other Side of Drowning" begins after her second ex-husband's drunk dial about his new lover and Yuknavitch's subsequent DUI. This memoir will leave you thought-struck and paralyzed with grief for the author, and for people who are going through difficult times.

◻ Expecting Adam:
A True Story of Birth, Rebirth, and Everyday Magic (1999)
by Martha Beck

••••••

It takes a certain kind of magic to write a memoir that is both a completely moving tearjerker and a riveting, laugh-out-loud romp. Martha and John Beck are knee-deep in Harvard academia when they learn that their expected child has Down syndrome. At first devastated, they make their way through the decisions and emotions one must move through when deciding to give birth and raise a child with a genetic disorder. When you gasp, shed a tear, and laugh on the same page, you know you have a winner. The quotation that has stuck with me in the years since I first read this book is this: "[T]he word *mother* is more powerful when it is used as a verb than as a noun. Mothering has little to do with biological reproduction—as another friend once told me, there are women who bear and raise children without ever mothering them, and there are people (both male and female) who mother all their lives without ever giving birth." I think I love this line so much because I decided long ago that I wasn't going to have children, but that doesn't stop me from mothering kids whom I'm lucky enough to know in this life.

House of Sand and Fog (1999)
by Andre Dubus III

••••••

You know those works of art that carve their initials on your insides and tear you limb from limb because you just know this is not going to end up okay? This is one of those books. And oh so glorious it is. Persian colonel Massoud Behrani, an immigrant desperate to find success in the United States, purchases a California bungalow. However, the sale was made due to a clerical error on the part of the county. The rightful owner of the bungalow is Kathy Nicolo, a former addict who is having an affair with a married cop. Nicolo is desperate to get her house back, the colonel is desperate to keep it, maddening misunderstandings take place, and mistakes are made that lead to an explosive ending.

The Invisible Bridge (2010)
by Julie Orringer

"It was like love, he thought, this crumbling chapel: it has been complicated, and therefore perfected, by what time had done to it."

••••••

After visiting Budapest on my honeymoon, I set out to read this novel, which is partially set in that beautiful city and tells of Hungary's role in World War II. In the book, Jewish architecture student Andras arrives in Paris with a letter he promised to deliver. However, he quickly becomes involved with the letter's recipient, and what emerges is the dark past of a family destroyed by the Holocaust. This plot-driven novel will stomp on your heart and linger well after you put it down.

◻ *It Gets Better:*
Coming Out, Overcoming Bullying,
and Creating a Life Worth Living (2011)
by Dan Savage and Terry Miller

●●●●●●

The It Gets Better Project exemplifies the power of social media. Sickened by news of LGBTQ teen suicides, Dan Savage and his husband Terry Miller set out to make a difference. They wanted to tell kids that getting through school was key, that no matter how awful things are at home or school, it does get better, they will find true friends, they will find acceptance, they will find love. Realizing it'd be near impossible to get speaking invitations to middle and high schools, the very places where homophobia does the most damage, Savage decided that he didn't need an invite—he didn't need permission to speak to the kids of today. Not in a world where Twitter, YouTube, and Facebook exist. Together, the authors recorded and posted their heartfelt "It Gets Better" video, hoping for a hundred similar videos from LGBTQ adults and straight allies. What they got instead were thousands of videos from everyday people, celebrities, companies, and politicians (including President Obama), and positive responses and thanks from teens and parents struggling with homophobic bullying. The impact it has made is truly inspirational. Read some of the messages in this book. I urge you to cry. I urge you to share a copy with a teen you know.

Lucky (1999)
by Alice Sebold

"I'll kill you if you scream . . . do you understand?"
I nodded my head. He released his hand from my
mouth. I screamed. Quickly. Abruptly.
The struggle began.

••••••

When author Alice Sebold was in college, she was brutally raped. While she was attacked, she fought with her fists, then with her words, then she curled up inside her head looking for poems and thinking of her mother until the horrible act was over. But of course this was just the beginning of her struggle. During the frustratingly frightening time when the police had no leads, Sebold was shocked to see her rapist on the street. She was able to lead police to him, but mistakes were made and it was a long journey into the courtroom. Interestingly, Sebold actually set out to write her bestselling novel *The Lovely Bones* first but hit a roadblock after the first chapter, in which the main character is raped and murdered. The author felt that she had to tell the story of her rape before being able to move on with the novel, so she stopped in order to write *Lucky*. In an interview, Sebold said, "[W]hereas in *Lovely Bones* the rape and murder scene was the first thing I wrote, in *Lucky* it was the last."

My Year of Meats (1998)
by Ruth L. Ozeki

*"There are many answers, none of them right,
but some of them most definitely wrong."*

• • • • • •

One of my favorite books of all time, this is the story of two women on opposite sides of the world who are loosely tied by Japanese culture, a book of prose (excerpts of which frame each chapter), and a weird documentary television series whose mission is to bring American meat into the homes of Japanese housewives. Meet Jane, the coordinator of the series, and Akiko, whose husband makes her watch it. At times a very funny book, it also has several cry-out-loud moments sprinkled throughout. The reader will also learn a lot of disturbing truths about how meat is produced in the United States.

◻ *PostSecret:*
Extraordinary Confessions from Ordinary Lives (2005)
by Frank Warren

•••••

What started as a blog in 2005 has become an international phenomenon with this book, and its sequels, art installations, controversy, and even a hoax involving the postcard admission of a murder. I read this entire book while standing in a bookstore. I laughed ("Sometimes when I do Chinese takeout, I order for 2 people so I won't look like a fat, lonely loser") and cried ("I love one of my children") without a care about what anyone thought of me. I think Frank Warren got it exactly right when he told an interviewer, "Every single person has at least one secret that would break your heart. If we could just remember this, I think there would be a lot more compassion and tolerance in the world."

Schindler's List (1982)
by Thomas Keneally

••••••

A novel based on true events, *Schindler's List,* originally titled *Schindler's Ark,* is about Oskar Schindler, a man who saved more Jews during the Holocaust than any other individual. From the author's note: "To use the texture and devices of a novel to tell a true story is a course that has frequently been followed in modern writing. It is the one I chose to follow here—both because the novelist's craft is the only one I can lay claim to, and because the novel's techniques seem suited for a character of such ambiguity and magnitude as Oskar. I have attempted, however, to avoid all fiction." The story behind how the book and subsequent film came to be is wonderful. According to Douglas Martin of the *New York Times,* Thomas Keneally had a chance encounter with Leopold Page (formerly Leopold Pfefferberg), a Holocaust survivor whom Schindler rescued. Upon finding out that Keneally was an author, Page spent forty-five minutes telling his story and showing the author all of the research he'd compiled about Schindler. Keneally not only agreed to write the book, but soon after it was published, Page began to pester Steven Spielberg into doing the film.

Tell the Wolves I'm Home (2012)
by Carol Rifka Brunt

••••••

June is a fourteen-year-old girl who would rather live in a magical place in a medieval time, but unfortunately she lives in New York City in the 1980s, and her beloved Uncle Finn has just died of AIDS. Devastated by his death, June has nowhere to turn, not to her sister, Greta, who is terribly mean to her, and not to her parents, who are busy with work and have their own issues. But after June meets a mysterious someone who was close to Finn, a person who understands her and actually wants to spend time with her, she finally begins the slow path through grief. Sincere and emotionally evocative without being melodramatic, this coming-of-age debut novel left me speechless with tears streaming down my cheeks. I think I even woke my husband up with my sniffles. "Are you crying?" he said. "Just reading," I answered, and he fell back asleep.

Chapter 11

Too Cool for School

Titles your high school English teacher should've assigned or maybe did, but you were skipping class that week.

I know so many American teenagers who are studious, ambitious readers, who have read way more classics than I did at their age. Some English teachers are inventive and (are allowed to) take a risk assigning something different than the usual stuff from the classic dead white straight dudes—Nathaniel Hawthorne, John Steinbeck, Ralph Waldo Emerson, Henry David Thoreau, William Faulkner, etc. Not that their books aren't important in their own right, of course. It's just that there is so much more out there that speaks to different experiences and perspectives. If you had one of those teachers who did assign something outside of the normal fifty or so books that appear on assigned reading lists every year, consider yourself lucky. If not, start with the following list.

The Awakening (1899)
by Kate Chopin

"[S]he tried to discover wherein this summer had been different from any and every other summer of her life. She could only realize that she herself—her present self—was in some way different from the other self. That she was seeing with different eyes and making the acquaintance of new conditions in herself that colored and changed her environment, she did not yet suspect."

••••••

A story about a woman reexamining her role as wife and mother and testing the boundaries of her marriage, *The Awakening* was not at all popular when it first came out in 1899. This is the earliest work of feminism I'd read (on my own) in high school and I was inspired to learn all that I could about the famous St. Louis author and her work. She became a personal hero of mine. She was so far ahead of her time that she didn't make much money from writing, and *The Awakening* even went out of print for many decades. During the production of the documentary *Kate Chopin: A Re-Awakening*, historian Elizabeth Fox-Genovese told producers Chopin was "a woman who took women extremely seriously. She never doubted women's ability to be strong." I think about Chopin a lot—when I visit my favorite St. Louis cemetery where she is buried, or when I see remnants of the 1904 World's Fair, which she attended, or when I think of a woman who is well ahead of her time.

☐ *Farewell to Manzanar:*
A True Story of Japanese American Experience During and After the World War II Internment (1972)
by Jeanne Wakatsuki Houston and James D. Houston

••••••

One of the more horrific events sanctioned by the United States government and many of its people was the internment of first-, second-, and third-generation Japanese Americans (and some German and Italian Americans) in 1942. It wasn't until a high school history teacher glossed over the topic that I learned what happened (and later I learned that another teacher in my school was a recipient of reparations in the late 1980s). One such incarceration camp was Manzanar, where 10,000 people were held, including Jeanne Wakatsuki Houston and her family, who were sent to the California camp when Jeanne was seven years old. I was surprised and inspired by their strength, defiance, and adaptability in the wave of fear and racism that swept over our country in the wake of Pearl Harbor. Today, Manzanar is a National Historic Site and the Manzanar Committee is a non-profit that has held an annual Manzanar Pilgrimage every April since 1969, which attracts students as well as internees and their families and friends.

Fences (1983)
by August Wilson

••••••

This Tony- and Pulitzer Prize–winning two-act play centers on Troy Maxson and his family as they struggle to establish roots as African Americans living in 1950s middle America. This is an interesting setting because the action takes place just before the major events of the Civil Rights Movement of the 1950s and 1960s. Although Troy is determined to be a better father to Cory than his sharecropper father was to him, he still has a long way to go. Cory feels that his father's reflexive suspicion of white people is holding him back, namely from a college football scholarship and a chance to make something of himself. The dialogue of the play mainly takes place around the building of a fence in their yard, the fence being a symbol for different things to the different characters—keeping in love, keeping others out, marking what belongs to us. In fact, it's the "fence" symbol from this play that has stuck with me over the years. Before the previous owners of our home could erect a privacy fence, an adjacent neighbor put up a length of fence that borders our backyard. The fence builders mistakenly thought they had a breezeway to the alley, so they installed a gate in the middle of the fence. When the property lines were determined and showed that there was no breezeway, the solution was to lock the gate we share with a padlock and throw away the key. When I first heard this story, I thought of Rose and Troy. That forever-locked gate seems to say, "You are uninvited. No one shall pass this arbitrary line. This piece of earth is mine, not yours." A fence is an interesting construct and I love that Wilson centered his play on one.

The Heart Is a Lonely Hunter (1940)
by Carson McCullers

● ● ● ● ● ●

John Singer, one of two mutes in a Georgia mill town, becomes a confidante for all of those who are lost, confused, or lonely. Much of the narrative centers on the struggles of four characters: a teenage tomboy who loves music, an African-American doctor, the owner of a diner, and a carny Marxist. All four believe they know what's going on behind Singer's facade, and all four feel that they are relating to him despite his inability to communicate. This is the "Island of Misfit Toys" of novels, which Carson McCullers wrote when she was just twenty-three years old.

The Importance of Being Earnest, *A Trivial Comedy for Serious People* (1895) by Oscar Wilde

••••••

Arguably Oscar Wilde's most enduring work, you should read this play about mistaken identities and English high society if only to be able to rightfully use the excuse of Bunburying in order to avoid social engagements. As in, "I'm very sorry I will miss the fundraiser, I must pay a visit to my friend Bunbury, who is in extraordinarily bad health." Or, "I cannot possibly read your book at this time, as my invalid friend Bunbury requires my assistance for a fortnight." Silly and filled with witty dialogue, this farcical play shines a light on the social conventions of the Victorian period, the human ego, and the complexity of family.

Johnny Got His Gun (1939)
by Dalton Trumbo

......

Although this brilliant and stark antiwar novel is set during World War I, it can easily speak to any war in human history. Joe is a soldier who has been severely maimed in an artillery blast. He awakens to realize that he is missing all of his limbs and most of his face, although his mind is completely and horrifyingly functioning. Joe is trapped inside his body. Through his internal dialogue and flashbacks of his past, readers are forced to participate in his grievous reawakening and acknowledge the human cost of war. The first time I read this, I read it late into the night, unable to sleep because I needed to see what was coming next. Like a car crash you pass on the highway, I just couldn't look away.

Man's Search for Meaning (1946)
by Viktor E. Frankl

"The salvation of man is through love and in love."

••••••

Although Dr. Viktor E. Frankl survived his imprisonment at Auschwitz between 1942 and 1945, his parents, brother, and pregnant wife were killed in concentration camps. But this book isn't a tale of desolation and sadness; it's a record of one man's determination to find meaning in the suffering. Dr. Frankl learned that life should not be about seeking pleasure or power, but should instead be a quest for meaning. The perspective this book offered me in college was a life changer and deeply affected my personal philosophy. My mantra after reading and processing this book is: surround yourself with positivity; if you are unhappy, change; make life meaningful to you and it will likely affect those around you and hence widen your circle of positivity.

◻ *Ordinary People* (1976)
by Judith Guest

*"They are ordinary people, after all. For a time they
had entered the world of the newspaper statistic;
a world where any measure you took to feel better
was temporary, at best, but that is over. This is
permanent. It must be."*

••••••

Stephen Chbosky's *The Perks of Being a Wallflower* meets J.D.
Salinger's *The Catcher in the Rye*: This book centers around
teenage Conrad Jarrett's battle with depression in the wake of
his older brother's accidental death. While Conrad gravitates
toward suicide, his mother's way of grieving is to wear a happy
mask and attempt to create and manage a perfectly organized,
perfectly controlled household. *Ordinary People* is an extraordinary piece of writing that examines grief and how it affects
loved ones differently.

The Outsiders (1967)
by S.E. Hinton

••••••

I find it amazing that S.E. Hinton was in high school when she wrote this book, one that is still assigned by the coolest teachers to teens year after year. It follows the rivalry between the Greasers and the Socs (pronounced after "Socials," not "socks" as I mistakenly thought when I first read it), but could easily be the story of any in-group versus out-group throughout time. I think that's why the book remains relevant to this day— everyone can relate. The film was very popular when I was young, and there was even a short-lived television spinoff. I love the characters' outlandish names: Ponyboy, Two-Bit, Sodapop, and Dally, to name a few.

Passing (1929)
by Nella Larsen

• • • • • •

Irene Redfield is a strong, successful, and giving mixed-race woman who lives in 1920s Harlem with her husband and children. When she encounters old childhood acquaintance Clare Kendry, who is also mixed-race, Irene instantly becomes fascinated and horrified because she learns that Clare has been passing as white. Clare has, in fact, married a white man who not only doesn't know she is of African-American ancestry, but also happens to be incredibly racist. At the same time Irene is intrigued by the life that Clare is living, Clare begins to contemplate the black culture she has been missing for many years. For more fantastic fiction about racial passing, see Kate Chopin's short story "Désirée's Baby" and check out Angela Nissel's memoir *Mixed: My Life in Black and White* (2006).

☐ *The Quiet American* (1955)
by Graham Greene

••••••

Alden Pyle is a talkative fool—in fact, as Robert Stone points out, "Pyle . . . illustrate[s] the joke's unspoken punch line: The only quiet American is a dead American." This book centers on Thomas Fowler, a drinking, opium-smoking, married British journalist who is living in 1954 Saigon with his Vietnamese mistress, Phuong. Pyle, the naive and loud American government worker sent to Saigon on a job, genuinely likes Fowler but is attracted to Phuong and thinks she deserves better. This love triangle is set against the disturbing backdrop of the conflict in Vietnam. Soon Fowler learns that Pyle isn't exactly who he appears to be and must decide whether to take action. Filled to the brim with compassion, loss, and paradox, just like war, this book came up on my radar when I was studying the Vietnam War.

Twelfth Night; or, What You Will (1623)
by William Shakespeare

••••••

Viola and Sebastian, twins separated from each other in a shipwreck, arrive independently in Illyria. Viola disguises herself as a boy called Cesario and enters the service of Duke Orsino, who is in love with the rich countess Olivia. Olivia rejects Orsino's advances but has a secret crush on Viola, believing her to be a man. A comedic sub-plot involves drunken revelry, more unrequited love, and a jester. And then Viola's twin brother comes on the scene turning everything on its head. This gender-bending romp of a comedy filled with mixed messages, mistaken identity, and madness is my favorite Shakespeare play.

Chapter 12

Tricksters, Fakers, and Cheats, Oh My!

Books about con artists and the people they scam.

My favorite college course was an English class called "The Art of the Con," where we read and discussed books and films about grifters, shills, tricks, schemes, and marks. The terminology from the world of confidence games is so fun! Con tricks are intriguing because they play on the human characteristics we value the most—trust, self-improvement, altruism, and a desire to connect with other people. They also bring out the very worst in us—gullibility, dishonesty, greed, naiveté, and desperation. This list includes nonfiction and fiction titles about the twisty world of the grift. They may even leave you suspicious of everyone you meet. Pull up your long game and revel in the dark world of confidence games.

American Gods (2001)
by Neil Gaiman

••••••

Mere days before being released from prison and being reunited with his beloved wife, Shadow learns that his wife and best friend are killed in an accident. Forlorn and lost in grief, he accepts a job as bodyguard and driver for Mr. Wednesday, a man who is not quite what he seems. Soon the dangerous and mysterious path down which Shadow travels teaches him that everyone has secrets, and that dreams (and nightmares) are real. Be sure to track down the tenth anniversary edition, which includes 12,000+ more words than the original and is Gaiman's preferred text.

◻ *The Big Con:*
The Story of the Confidence Man (1940)
by David W. Maurer

"O.K.," says John. "We'll give him the hides.
What kind of an egg is he?"
"Well, he's no lop-eared mark," says Jimmy.
"He knows what it is all about. And he may be hard
to handle. He is a hefty baby with plenty of moxie.
I'd guess he'll be hard to cool out."
"If he gets fractious, he'll get the cackle-bladder.
That cools out those tough babies.
Do you want to find the poke for him?"

••••••

The Big Con was written by a linguist who was fascinated
with and spent much of his time studying criminal dialects—
particularly the language of the confidence man. This infinitely
entertaining, timeless work of criminology includes detailed
descriptions of how each game is carried out and the historical
characters involved (including Barney the Patch and Limehouse
Chappie), as well as a glossary.

◻ *Catch Me If You Can:*
The True Story of a Real Fake (1980)
by Frank W. Abagnale

●●●●●●

The first I ever heard of this fascinating imposter turned FBI consultant was in my high school criminology class when Mr. Rinderknecht played a sound recording of Frank Abagnale telling about his exploits as a (fake) pilot, professor, attorney, and doctor, all of which occurred between the ages of sixteen and twenty-one. Throughout the book, Abagnale never really provided reasons for his many stunts, except to say that he impersonated a pilot because they were respected and he just wanted to fly around the world for free. His story was turned into a film and a Broadway musical, and Abagnale has since published several books on, you guessed it, how to protect yourself from identity theft.

☐ *The Confidence-Man:*
His Masquerade (1857)
by Herman Melville

• • • • • •

Confession: when I first read this book, I was confused and later furious, and all because this book about a con man is actually a trick on the reader. I don't think telling you this is a spoiler, because the story takes place on April 1. And it's a great ruse because, as editor Stephen Matterson writes in the introduction to one edition of *The Confidence-Man*, "the confidence trick depended upon the trust of the victim"—when else are we as completely trusting as we are after sitting down, getting cozy, and opening a book? This famous book is thought to be a parody on Plato's *Republic*.

◻ *The Gentle Grafter* (1907)
by O. Henry

● ● ● ● ● ●

The Gentle Grafter is a collection of stories about grifters and graft by short story master O. Henry, who penned "The Gift of the Magi." It includes such stories as "The Chair of Philanthromathematics," "The Exact Science of Matrimony," and "Shearing the Wolf." My favorite, however, is a story called "Conscience in Art," about two con men with very different philosophies: Peter prefers to leave something with those he cons rather than outright stealing from them, and Andy takes, takes, takes without looking back. Their differences come into play during the Henry signature twist ending of this story about a con on a Pittsburgh art dealer. This collection is O. Henry at his cleverest!

The Good Thief (2008)
by Hannah Tinti

••••••

Ren is a one-handed orphan with a mysterious past. One day a man named Benjamin Nab arrives at his orphanage with a fantastic story, claiming to be the boy's older brother. Ren is doubtful of the story but goes away with Benjamin just the same. He soon learns that the man is a con man eager for a sympathy-evoking sidekick to help him swindle and steal his way across the countryside. And what a frightening, bloody journey it is! I'm including this book in this list not only because it's a great book full of trickery, but because it was another one of those books I started before bed and didn't close until I was finished, in the darkest part of the night. It's absolutely entrancing.

The Grifters (1963)
by Jim Thompson

"There was one thing about playing the angles. If you played them long enough, you knew the other guy's as well as you knew your own. Most of the time it was like you were looking out the same window."

• • • • • •

Roy Dillon is a charming crook who makes a living doing short cons while his mother Lilly is a seasoned con artist who loves the long game of racetrack swindling. But Roy is at a turning point in his life—is it time to move on from the life of crime, or should he fully embrace his upbringing? The descriptions and variety of the cons presented in this book are fascinating! The reason I got into Thompson in the first place was after reading an interview with Stephen King in which he said of Thompson, "He was crazy. He went running into the American subconscious with a blowtorch in one hand and a pistol in the other, screaming his goddamn head off. No one else came close."

◻︎ *Invisible* (2009)
by Paul Auster

●●●●●●

The novel opens as Adam Walker, a student, meets visiting professor Rudolf Born and his live-in girlfriend Margot in 1967. Before long, Walker finds that he has become entangled in a random, dramatic incident involving Born and Margot that alters the course of his life. The story is told by three different narrators in three different locales from 1967 to 2007—in an effort, I think, to throw the reader into a whirlwind of questions about trust, obsession, desperation, and how memory clouds what is fact and what is fiction. Be warned, this novel is the king of unreliable narration.

The Lies of Locke Lamora (2006)
by Scott Lynch

*"We're a different sort of thief here, Lamora.
Deception and misdirection are our tools. We don't
believe in hard work when a false face and a good line
of bullshit can do so much more."*

••••••

Locke Lamora is a witty, thieving, foul-mouthed orphan who joins an eyeless priest's group of swindler orphans called the Gentlemen Bastards. Soon Locke is the leader of the Bastards and together they con nearly everyone in the island city of Camorr, including the feared ruler of the criminal underworld. Enter other players in the dangerous game of greed and fantasy. I especially appreciate the hilarious dialogue, clever characterizations, and inventive insults. This is the first book of the Gentlemen Bastards series.

◻ *The Mark Inside:*
A Perfect Swindle, a Cunning Revenge,
and a Small History of the Big Con (2012)
by Amy Reading

•••••

Author Amy Reading reveals the ins and outs of the big con and its presence throughout history against the backdrop of the story about a con that occurred in 1919. J. Frank Norfleet, a middle-aged Texas rancher, was swindled in a stock market scam by a group of con artists—not once but twice. So he spent the next four years roaming around the country, pretending to be a naive country boy and allowing himself to be approached by different con artists in order to gather evidence against his enemies and exact revenge, while at the same time out-conning the con men he was meeting. Reading does an impressive amount of research for this book, which includes a note on her methodology, photos, and a bibliography of almost 250 sources.

☐ *Matchstick Men:*
A Novel about Grifters with Issues (2002)
by Eric Garcia

• • • • • •

Roy and Frankie are partners in crime and have been perfect-
ing the short and long con games together for years. They have
chemistry, ambition, and grit, but they also have issues. Roy
suffers from obsessive-compulsive disorder and has recently discovered he has a teenage daughter who, he soon learns, is inter-
ested in the family business. Frankie is annoyed by the presence
of Roy's daughter and is looking forward to the next big con. I
read this entire book on a cross-country plane ride and found
the present tense narration to be a nice change of pace that
made the story zip right along to its shocking finale.

My Heart Laid Bare (1998)
by Joyce Carol Oates

*"The Game is never to be played as if it
were but a game when it is in fact life."*

● ● ● ● ● ●

A fascinating departure for Oates is this sweeping period piece set in 1890s America. Abraham Licht is the patriarch of a family of swindlers who don't seek to make money so much as they seek to master "The Game" as they play from New York to D.C. and back again. This book is as unlike Oates's other books as Stephen King's *The Eyes of the Dragon* differs from his usual horror fests. That said, I urge you to seek out any of Oates's other books and short stories as well!

◻ *Parlor Games* (2013)
by Maryka Biaggio

"And, after all, men are not terribly difficult
to manage. They are rather like puppies:
Roll them on their back and convince them you're
master and you've tamed them."

• • • • • •

This historical novel is based on the true story of the most famous and seductive female con artist, May Dugas. The story bounces from her 1917 trial to flashbacks of her scams to the multinational steadfast pursuit of her by the Pinkerton Agency, which dubbed her "the most dangerous woman." May's voice is seductive, glib, and crafty. I found myself utterly bewitched by May as I was reading. This book, told in first person, reads like a radio show.

Chapter 13

Very Truly Yours

Books written in the form of letters, e-mail, diary entries, and more.

For those of us who love letter writing and receiving, the epistolary genre is a dream come true. Typically stories written in the form of correspondence, they can also be stories made up of newspaper clippings, blog posts, e-mail or text messages, transcripts, diary entries, or a mix. In epistolary books there isn't a narrator; there are one or more (sometimes unreliable) perspectives instead. The tone is usually casual, the language heavy on the vernacular, and the story told from a much more subjective viewpoint than an omniscient narration. Readers are dropped right in the middle of a conversation, and usually the epistolary form chosen almost becomes a character in itself. The epistolary novel is an old-fashioned genre that is making a comeback in a big way.

☐ *84, Charing Cross Road* (1970)
by Helene Hanff

● ● ● ● ● ●

A love letter to books, this title could just as easily be in the "Meta Textuals" chapter. The true story of Helene Hanff's friendship with British antiquarian bookseller Frank Doel unfolds via letters exchanged between the two over twenty years during the 1950s and 1960s. The letters are so fun to read because Hanff is a spirited, blunt New Yorker and Doel is a polite and reserved Englishman. There is a full list of the books Hanff ordered on the Wikipedia page for *84, Charing Cross Road*. A fascinating assortment! What I enjoy about this book is that it is genre-defying: It's part memoir, part world history, and part literary criticism.

Almost Like Being in Love (2004)
by Steve Kluger

••••••

Probably the most epistolary of them all, this story of the reunion between thirty-eight-year-old Travis and his former high school sweetheart Craig is told through a series of letters, journal entries, fake obituaries (yes, fake), checklists, bulletin board notes, menus, school assignments, Internet search results, and newspaper articles. Craig, former high school jock turned lawyer, is about to marry a long-term boyfriend but is having misgivings, especially when thoughts of his first love, Travis, come to mind. Travis, the theatre-loving professor, has been unlucky in love pretty much since high school. This sweet, funny, and utterly quotable book can easily be read in one sitting but may make you contemplate all of your previous lovers.

⬜ *The Collector* (1963)
by John Fowles

"I think we are just insects,
we live a bit and then die and that's the lot.
There's no mercy in things.
There's not even a Great Beyond. There's nothing."

● ● ● ● ● ●

The Collector is one of the first truly haunting books I read. Frederick Clegg stalked and kidnapped Miranda Grey and has imprisoned her in his basement. The story alternates between the viewpoints of Miranda Grey and her captor. From Clegg's observations and Grey's diary entries, readers learn the tactics Grey uses to try to escape, and how truly sadistic Clegg is. Don't read this book late into the night or you won't be able to sleep.

Dangerous Liaisons (1782)
by Pierre Choderlos de Laclos

••••••

Any book that is deemed scandalous throughout the ages is okay in my, ahem, book. De Laclos takes the epistolary form and uses it beautifully in this story of aristocratic corruption, sadistic seduction, and the manipulative games played by ex-lovers the Marquise de Merteuil and the Vicomte de Valmont. Each letter presented is crucial to the plot advancement, and the letters almost become a character in and of themselves. I first stumbled across this book in college and loved it for its dark and twisty look at the French aristocracy. De Laclos reminds me of a cross between Jonathan Swift and Dante in this work that holds a mirror up to society's ugly bits.

☐ *Dracula* (1897)
by Bram Stoker

••••••

I'd of course heard about *Dracula* before I read it, and what came to mind was vampires, stakes, crucifixes, the names of the main characters Jonathan and Mina Harker. But there are three things of which I was wholly unaware before I read it: *Dracula* is a book about sex (bisexuality, homoeroticism, gender bending, repression, and sexual power); *Dracula* is an epistolary novel, told in the form of letters and journal entries; and *Dracula* was not a hit during Stoker's time. In fact, according to his article in the *Guardian*, pop culture historian Christopher Frayling wrote that when Stoker died in 1912, his obituaries "scarcely mentioned *Dracula* at all. Today, they would mention little else." Another famous classic written in this form is also another favorite, Mary Shelley's *Frankenstein* (1818).

Ella Minnow Pea:
A Progressively Lipogrammatic Epistolary Fable
(also known as *Ella Minnow Pea: A Novel in Letters*) (2001)
by Mark Dunn

"'Love one another, push the perimeter of this glorious
language. Lastly, please show proper courtesy; open not
your neighbor's mail.'"

••••••

Ella Minnow Pea is set in Nollop, a fictional island off the coast of South Carolina founded by the man who coined the sentence that uses each letter of the English alphabet "The quick brown fox jumps over the lazy dog." This story is progressively lipogrammatic, a lipogram being writing that forbids the use of certain letters. It's told exclusively in the form of letters between citizens of the town, including a girl named Ella Minnow Pea. This delightful fable is a love letter to wordsmiths and alphabeticians.

Flowers for Algernon (1959)
by Daniel Keyes

*"Now I understand that one of the important reasons
for going to college and getting an education is to
learn that the things you've believed in all your life
aren't true, and that nothing is what it appears to be."*

••••••

Thirty-two-year-old Charlie Gordon has an intellectual dis-ability, but thanks to a new radical procedure already tested on a mouse named Algernon, doctors and scientists are able to reverse his condition and Charlie is able to gain more knowl-edge and intelligence than he ever imagined possible. But when the mouse's health begins to decline, everyone involved won-ders if Charlie's will follow the same path. This fascinating story is told via Charlie's diary entries.

Fried Green Tomatoes at the Whistle Stop Cafe (1987)
by Fannie Flagg

••••••

This imaginative novel weaves together the past and the present, beginning with the developing friendship between Ninny Threadgoode, an elderly nursing home resident, and an unhappy middle-aged woman named Evelyn Couch who comes to visit her. During each visit, Mrs. Threadgoode shares more about the remarkable events that took place in Depression-era Whistle Stop, Alabama, home of Dot Weems's weekly column (the main epistolary device) and the then-new Whistle Stop Cafe run by Idgie Threadgoode and Ruth Jamison. The narration and time periods change throughout the book, but there are visual clues at the beginning of each chapter to aid the reader. This book is full of witty, colorful language and hilarity, but I especially like the darker story line hidden within.

Griffin and Sabine:
An Extraordinary Correspondence (1991)
by Nick Bantock

"Foolish man. You cannot turn me into
a phantom because you are frightened.
You do not dismiss a muse at a whim."

••••••

I can't tell whether this title and its five sequels, some of the few books I actually own, are more books or works of book art. And I'm sorry to say that I think it'll be difficult to find these at a public library, because between the pages are envelopes with slips of paper, real removable postcards, and beautiful, sometimes disturbing, illustrations. What is revealed is either a mysterious blossoming love story or a solitary artist's developing madness. You'll definitely want the whole series on hand as you jump from cliffhanger to cliffhanger.

The Gum Thief (2007)
by Douglas Coupland

●●●●●●

Meet Roger, a bored, middle-aged sales associate at Staples who drinks at work, and Bethany, a teenage goth girl who hates her job. One day, Bethany finds Roger's diary in which he is pretending to be Bethany, and they start writing back and forth to each other, all the while acting like nothing at all has changed among themselves and the terminally clueless dopes with whom they work. This book humorously and poignantly underlines the fact that people of the most disparate backgrounds and lives can connect meaningfully, or at least out of desperation.

☐ *In the Time of the Butterflies* (1994)
by Julia Alvarez

••••••

Patria, Minerva, and María Teresa were the real-life Mirabal sisters who spoke out against Rafael Trujillo, the longtime dictator of the Dominican Republic. Despite all of the horror he imposed on his people, it wasn't until he gave orders to have the Mirabal sisters assassinated on a fateful day in 1960 that change really took place. This account of the sisters, at times first person from the sisters' points of view and at times third person, is fictionalized. Fittingly, when a New York school board banned this title for containing a diagram of a bomb, two students stood up and spoke out against the challenge—illustrating that they truly understood the message behind this story.

A Woman of Independent Means (1978)
by Elizabeth Forsythe Hailey

●●●●●●

Elizabeth (Bess) Alcott Steed is a woman of independent means. Told exclusively via letters sent by Bess between 1899 and 1968, to family members and to her husband Robert when they were apart, this is a story of a fiercely curious, funny, self-sufficient, adventurous woman well ahead of her time. When Bess comes into an inheritance, a contract for the repayment of a loan granted to her husband appears in the pages. I love that she's as responsible for his success as he is. Hailey, also a journalist and a playwright, has said that Bess was inspired by the life of her grandmother.

◻ *Youth in Revolt:*
The Journals of Nick Twisp (1993)
by C.D. Payne

"I have found that people who can successfully resist
temptation invariably lead depressingly stunted lives."

••••••

This big old 498-page book is six months' worth of journal entries written by Nick Twisp, a hyper-nerdy teenage virgin obsessed with sex. Laugh out loud alongside him as he copes hilariously with his parents' divorce, the trials and tribulations of high school, and how in the world he can win over Sheeni Saunders, goddess of intellect. For a goofy ride through teenage nerd-dom, you can't get much better than this title and its many sequels, which can be read in order or stand on their own.

Chapter 14

What Not to Read While Drinking Milk

Humorous fiction, memoirs, and essays that will make milk squirt from your nose.

There is laughter therapy, laughter yoga, and laughter meditation. There is a whole branch of science dedicated to the study of the health benefits of laughter (gelotology). Humor books are some of the most popular books out there. And there is nothing better than being on an airplane while the person next to you is reading a laugh-out-loud book while trying to contain his or her giggles—except maybe being the one who's reading it! This chapter contains some of the funniest books I recommend, from titles by comedians and those who've had goofy childhoods to novels that sneak up and smack your funny bone.

There is no need for a laugh track, a tickle from a feather, or an Internet cat meme; these books contain pages upon pages of good old-fashioned belly laughs. Go ahead and reach for one of these hilarious books, guaranteed to make you almost wet your pants. It's good for you.

The Absolutely True Diary of a Part-Time Indian (2007)
by Sherman Alexie

"I grabbed my book and opened it up. I wanted to smell it. Heck, I wanted to kiss it. Yes, kiss it. That's right, I am a book kisser. Maybe that's kind of perverted or maybe it's just romantic and highly intelligent. *"*

••••••

Disclaimer: this book is easily one of the funniest books I've ever read, but it also qualifies as a tearjerker. That's because everything that makes you laugh about Junior's life is also completely depressing. Junior knows how limiting life can be on the Spokane Indian Reservation—he was born sickly, he's attended more funerals than most people attend in a lifetime, and he's been bullied for most of his fourteen years. Now he's being called an "apple" (red on the outside, white on the inside), among other things, for deciding to attend an all-white school off the rez. Through his diary and drawings, we learn that his biggest coping mechanism is his talent as a budding cartoonist and his desire to be better than poor.

Born Standing Up:
A Comic's Life (2007)
by Steve Martin

"At first I was not famous enough, then I was too famous,
now I am famous just right. Oh yes, I have heard the
argument that celebrities want fame when it's useful and
don't when it's not. That argument is absolutely true."

••••••

Steve Martin was a television staple in my childhood home. Little did I know that he was also a stand-up comedian, author, magician, screenwriter, producer, and playwright—and, at age ten, a peddler of guidebooks at the newly opened Disneyland. This memoir hilariously touches on different parts of his expansive career and then tenderly discusses the downside of fame and the grief he experienced over his strained familial relationships and the eventual deaths of his parents. Steve Martin is a multifaceted wonder.

☐ *Bossypants* (2011)
by Tina Fey

"My ability to turn good news into anxiety is rivaled only by my ability to turn anxiety into chin acne."

●●●●●●

Tina Fey is one of my favorite comedians. In *Bossypants*, Fey take a hilarious look back at her time with an improv group at Second City, her tenure with *Saturday Night Live*, and the creation of her popular show *30 Rock* with self-reflection and self-deprecation. And I love that it's not all humor: Fey brilliantly includes social commentary on the blatant sexism that goes on in the world of comedy, and there is a rich chapter in there about her relationship with her father and how he impacted her life. Be warned: Fey reads the audio version of the book, and I almost got into an accident while listening to it because I was laughing so hard, no joke.

A Girl Named Zippy:
Growing Up Small in Mooreland, Indiana (2001)
by Haven Kimmel

• • • • • •

Haven Kimmel, nicknamed Zippy by her father, was born bald and didn't utter a word until age two years and eight months when her dad told her it was time to give up the bottle. At that moment, she turned to him, pulled the bottle out of her mouth and offered her first words: "I'll make a deal with you . . . if you let me keep it, I'll hide it when company comes and I won't tell no-body." Behold the stories of Zippy and her family! The vignettes are the perfect length and style for reading out loud or on the toilet, or maybe out loud from the toilet. Tremendously funny and tender, *Zippy* is one of my favorite books.

Hypocrite in a Pouffy White Dress: Tales of Growing Up Groovy and Clueless (2005) by Susan Jane Gilman

*"When I was little, I was so girlie and ambitious,
I was practically a drag queen. I wanted to be
everything at once: a prima ballerina, an actress,
a model, a famous artist, a nurse, an Ice Capades
dancer, and Batgirl. I spent inordinate amounts of
time waltzing around our living room with a doily
on my head, imagining in great detail my promenade
down the runway as the new Miss America, during
which time I would also happen to receive a Nobel
Prize for coloring."*

••••••

For the feminist who loves to wear tutus, this memoir of growing up as a Manhattanite and daughter of hippie parents is sure to please. I remember reading a portion of this book in my break room when I worked in retail. I got the stink eye from my coworkers as they watched soap operas because of my raucous laughter and snorting. Susan Jane Gilman breaks her book into three parts: childhood, teenager/young adult, and adulthood. My favorite is the first of the three.

The Idiot Girls' Action-Adventure Club:
True Tales from a Magnificent and Clumsy Life (2002)
by Laurie Notaro

••••••

Laurie Notaro regales us with her hilarious misadventures in the form of autobiographical vignettes in the style of David Sedaris. The stories feature tons of drinking, cussing, self-deprecating humor (my favorite), and lessons about creepster boyfriends and menstruation. My very favorite story involves Laurie taking her grandfather, Pop Pop, to the grocery store. He insists that she drive around back to look for day-old bread in the dumpster and they hit the jackpot: a solitary shopping cart filled with expired baked goods. Suddenly, her grandfather is fit as a fiddle as he leaps out to fill his arms, and Laurie's backseat, with the bounty. When a huge delivery truck begins backing up too close to Laurie's car, she has no choice but to hit the gas in order to move a few feet away. "But I guess a couple of feet was all it took to drag my grandfather—who despite the mortal severity of the situation could not interrupt his heist for two to three seconds—almost to the ground. I gasped when I saw him get knocked over by the car, but he got right back up and tossed another cheesecake into the backseat." I can just picture this entire scenario, and every time I read it I nearly fall to the ground myself. This is Notaro's finest collection of stories.

The Internet Is a Playground:
Irreverent Correspondences of an Evil Online Genius (2011)
by David Thorne

*"I find that loud music helps me relax while I clean,
because the music distracts me so much that I stop
cleaning. Which is relaxing."*

••••••

David Thorne uses the Internet for all the right reasons: humor and humor. This book is a quick and fun way to spend an afternoon—it's chock-full of comical online encounters, lists of goofy things his son has said, types of monkeys it'd be nice to have, and a step-by-step guide to buying a sofa from IKEA. Find all of his trollish antics at *www.27bslash6.com* and be glad if you do not live near, work with, or have any connection at all to Thorne!

Let's Explore Diabetes with Owls (2013)
by David Sedaris

"I don't know how these couples do it, spend hours each night tucking their kids in, reading them books about misguided kittens or seals who wear uniforms, and then rereading them if the child so orders. In my house, our parents put us to bed with two simple words: 'Shut up.'"

●●●●●●

Let's Explore Diabetes with Owls is another fabulous book of observations, interpretations, and musings by America's quirkiest fellow. If and when you meet David Sedaris at a book signing, let me know what he says to you and how he inscribes the book. He has a reputation for saying strange things at signings to keep himself from being bored! I can't tell you what he said to my friend Britta at a library conference in 2014—it's way too weird—but a Twitter friend snapped a picture of the inscription he got from Sedaris. It reads, "To Chip, Why did you let them kill me?" next to a drawing of Jesus (maybe).

Letters from a Nut (1997)
by Ted L. Nancy

●●●●●●

Ted L. Nancy is a highly original prankster. His shtick is writing different companies, celebrities, politicians, and organizations with completely ridiculous messages of complaint, praise, or inquiry and then sharing both the letter and its response. The responses are just as funny because usually they are written in earnest. One such response from the famous bus line was: "On behalf of Greyhound Lines, I would like to advise you there should be no problem traveling while in your butter costume." Ted L. Nancy is the pseudonym of comedian Barry Marder. There are several sequels to this book as well as a children's book spinoff, *Letters from a Nut's Family Tree* (2013), which contain letters purportedly written by the author's ancestors. A comedic genius!

Little Failure: A Memoir (2014)
by Gary Shteyngart

"Let's start with my surname: Shteyngart. A German name whose insane Sovietized spelling, eye-watering bunching of consonants (just one i *between the* h *and* t *and you got some pretty nice 'Shit' there), and overall unattractiveness has cost me a lot of human warmth. 'Mr., uh, I can't pronounce this . . .* Shit . . . Shit . . . Shitfart?'"

●●●●●●

From the author of *Super Sad True Love Story* (2010) comes this delectably entertaining memoir about a Jewish Russian who immigrates to America when he is seven years old. The book contains adorable photos of Shteyngart and family, including photos of his mother, who coined the English-Russian fusion word "Failurchka" (*little failure*) to lovingly describe her son. At times tender, this book packs a wallop of laugh-out-loud moments.

Sh*t My Dad Says (2010)
by Justin Halpern

●●●●●●

Justin Halpern's dad on packing a school lunch: "You have to pack a sandwich. It can't just be cookies and bullshit . . . No, I said if you packed it yourself, you could pack it how you want, not pack it like a moron." I heart Justin Halpern's dad! This book (rather, a Twitter feed turned bestselling book turned failed TV show) is the true story of a twenty-something who is again living with his parents after just being dumped by his girlfriend. Justin started a Twitter profile to record all of the hilarious and philosophical musings made by his dad, a man who is unapologetically gruff, direct, crude, and ultimately loving, honest, and genuine.

◻ *Then We Came to the End* (2007)
by Joshua Ferris

"We loved killing time and had perfected several ways
of doing so. We wandered the hallways carrying papers
that indicated some mission of business when in
reality we were in search of free candy."

• • • • • •

The office is falling apart. Coworkers are being laid off one by one, the only meaningful work left is an unusual pro-bono ad campaign, an office chair goes hilariously missing, paranoia and gossip and office pranks are rampant, and Tom Mota is wearing three polo shirts at the same time. Ferris is a master at witty, casual, utterly believable dialogue. True story, I did a stint in an office one time. One day, bored out of my mind, I decided to conduct a sociological experiment involving a new bowl of candy that I placed on a filing cabinet just outside my office door. Depending on what sort of candy was in the bowl, people would take a piece and quickly make themselves scarce, or they would spend time rooting around a bit. It turned out a Tootsie Roll mix was the perfect way to get people to congregate outside your office so you can eavesdrop on them as they spilled the not-so-juicy but better-than-nothing office gossip. It helped to pass the time for a few days.

Yes Man (2005)
by Danny Wallace

••••••

Danny Wallace likes to do weird things, such as finding enough people who share his roommate's name to fill a deck of cards (see the 2002 book *Are You Dave Gorman?*), starting a random-act-of-kindness cult (see the 2003 book *Join Me!*), and, as documented in this book, taking a stranger's advice to say yes more often and turning it into a rule he follows for six months. And what funny adventures he has! Unexpected trips, correspondence with spammers, drugs in Amsterdam, connections with strangers. Of course some of the yeses are silly, and he doesn't advise readers to follow his lead, but he points out the transformative power of the word and how it truly impacted his frame of mind and bestowed upon him opportunities he never thought possible. For other delightfully gimmicky reads, also check out A.J. Jacobs's series of "One Man's Humble Quest" books, including *Drop Dead Healthy: One Man's Humble Quest for Bodily Perfection* (2012) and *The Year of Living Biblically: One Man's Humble Quest to Follow the Bible as Literally as Possible* (2007).

Chapter 15
YA for the Not So YA

Young adult books that everyone will dig.

There is no official age range for young adult (YA) literature. Some say it's twelve to eighteen; others extend it to age twenty-five. That said, there is absolutely nothing wrong with reading outside of your age range. Over the years of working in a library, I've noticed more and more adults becoming comfortable "shopping" out of the teen section. Don't let a publisher's label keep you from reading good books—think of it as an indicator of how youthful the book will make you feel. Open a YA book and discover the Fountain of Youth. From reinvented fairy tales to stories of first love and loss, these are teen books every adult should read.

Beauty: A Retelling of the Story of Beauty and the Beast (1978)
by Robin McKinley

"I always get my own way in the end, Papa."

••••••

Fairy tale retellings are compelling—taking something well-known and turning it on its head. This one is about Beauty, a girl whose nickname doesn't quite match up with reality, but whose spirit, intelligence, and courage make up for any problem in the looks department. She immediately volunteers to surrender herself to the enchanted beast to atone for an error made by her father. If you get it in your head that the Disney version is somehow better or similar, please note that McKinley's novel came out thirteen years before Disney's movie. I sought out the traditional tale written by Jeanne-Marie Leprince de Beaumont in 1756 and then gave this one a reread. I fell in love with the relationship between the sisters, and of course, that between Beauty and the beast.

□ *Cold Hands, Warm Heart* (2009)
by Jill Wolfson

••••••

When we were teenagers, my best friend's sister had a liver transplant. Kim's liver failure was swift, there was no extended illness, and her need was so dire that she was shot to the top of the list and was lucky enough to receive an organ within a couple of days. I think that's why this book, about young people and organ transplants, resonated so much with me. Meet fifteen-year-old Dani, who just wants to pierce her ears and skip school and eat junk food like other girls her age, except for the fact she was born with a weak heart on the wrong side of her chest. She is now at the top of the transplant list as Recipient #6211. Tired all the time, pale as snow, with cold hands, two weeks from death, Dani is waiting for somebody's someone to die so that she can have a working heart. And then it happens. Tyler's sister Amanda suffers a freak gymnastics accident that leaves her brain-dead, and her heart is a perfect match for Dani. After the surgery, Dani yearns to know more about the heart inside her and the person from whom it came, and she struggles with the feeling that maybe she doesn't deserve the gift. Reading this beautiful tale about a delicate subject, I found myself laughing aloud, sobbing, and utterly grateful for the people I love.

The Disreputable History of Frankie Landau-Banks (2008)
by E. Lockhart

*"Matthew had called her harmless. Harmless. And
being with him made Frankie feel squashed into a
box—a box where she was expected to be sweet and
sensitive (but not oversensitive); a box for young and
pretty girls who were not as bright or powerful as their
boyfriends. A box for people who were not forces to be
reckoned with. Frankie wanted to be a force."*

●●●●●●

Frankie Landau-Banks is strong, fierce, and smarter than most
of the boys in her boyfriend's all-male secret society. And she
yearns to be included in the club that wreaks havoc and carries
out pranks at their New England prep school. But instead of
creating her own secret society, or giving up, she seeks to not
only infiltrate his, but overtake it. Amid capers and takeovers is
schoolwork, and Frankie learns all that she can about feminism,
sociology, panopticons, and surveillance, which may all be useful when the time comes. E. Lockhart is my favorite YA author,
so it's fitting that my favorite YA character of all time is Frankie
Landau-Banks.

◻ *Eleanor & Park* (2012)
by Rainbow Rowell

••••••

Misfits unite in this poignant tale of an unexpected first high school love. Park, meet Eleanor, a poor, new-to-school transfer student who lives with her dysfunctional family. Eleanor, meet Park, a Korean American who tries his best to stay under the radar, despite being the only Asian-American kid at school. The chapters of the book alternate between the perspectives of the two as they struggle to make their relationship work despite the odds. Adults will love the references to 1980s mix tapes and the maudlin music that filled them. Check out the audiobook, which is just as great as the book.

◻ *Geography Club* (2003)
by Brent Hartinger

••••••

Russel Middlebrook is your average high school student, except that he's gay and keeping it a secret. Surrounded by people but lonely, Russel agrees to meet with someone he hooked up with in a gay chat room. When Russel discovers that his chat mate is Kevin Land, a popular boy on his high school's baseball team, he realizes that for the first time in his life, he "was friends with a) one of the most popular kids in school, and b) an actual gay person." Soon they connect with other gay and bisexual classmates and form a fake club in order to have an excuse to meet. The Geography Club soon becomes a safe and welcoming space for the students. This is the first title in the Russel Middlebrook series of books and has also been adapted into a play and a film.

◻ *The Haunting of Alaizabel Cray* (2001)
by Chris Wooding

*"We may choose our own paths, but the pattern
is always ahead of us. It is a way. It is the way."*

••••••

A young adult fantasy in four parts, this book centers on seventeen-year-old wych-hunters Thaniel and Cathaline as they track weird and creepy creatures like ghouls, Cradlejacks, and other wych-kin, in an alternate post-gothic London. The stories of hunting, a possessed girl, and a serial killer intertwine, creating a chilly and dark nightmare world—what I wouldn't give to get a peek into Wooding's brain! This is a fun, action-packed, fast-paced steampunk fantasy that adults will love.

◻ *Jellicoe Road* (2006)
by Melina Marchetta

••••••

My favorite line from this heartfelt book about a girl with a mysterious past: "I remember love. It's what I have to keep on reminding myself. It's funny how you can forget everything except people loving you. Maybe that's why humans find it so hard getting over love affairs. It's not the pain they're getting over, it's the love." Seventeen-year-old Taylor Markham is one of the leaders of her Australian boarding school and she may have developed a thing for a rival leader, Jonah. Jonah may be able to shed some light on why Taylor's mom abandoned her six years earlier. Their connection might also reveal the origin of the rival school factions. When people make fun of teen fiction for being all vampires and vanilla girl characters, I present them with *Jellicoe Road*. I will say that we teen services librarians loved this Printz Award–winning book more than our teen patrons did because of the slow, lyrical buildup.

□ *King Dork* (2006)
by Frank Portman

●●●●●●

Besides having one of the best book covers ever, this book is for music lovers, nerds, those who can't stand *The Catcher in the Rye*, and everyone in between. When Tom, King Dork, finds his deceased father's copy of the classic book and the margin notes contained within, it sparks a year-long investigation into his father's (murder? suicide?) death. Along the way, he also discovers that being in a band could be the secret to getting laid. Managing to write a book that is hilarious but at times serious and painful is no easy feat, and this one even comes with a goofy glossary and a bandography to boot. Beware: if you listen to the audiobook while driving, you might laugh yourself right off the road.

The Lover's Dictionary (2010)
by David Levithan

••••••

I once attended a non-librarian conference in San Francisco on marketing to youth, which David Levithan also attended. My being the only librarian there meant that David Levithan did not have a hoard of admirers surrounding him at the cocktail party after his panel discussion, so of course I wandered up to him and acted as if I had no idea who he was just so I could have a conversation with him without having to reveal the annoying librarian author crush I had. (Side note: he is a very kind and gracious fellow.) Then this book came out and I almost died. Tiny vignettes, some no longer than a line, will take hold of you and lead you through the alphabet, through the land of dating and sex and love and loss, in a format as fractured as love itself.

◻ *Monster* (1999)
by Walter Dean Myers

● ● ● ● ● ●

African-American teen Steve Harmon is in jail for allegedly par-
ticipating in the robbery of a convenience store in Harlem that
resulted in the death of the store owner. The story reads like a
screenplay—as if Steve is on the outside looking in as he preps
for his lawyer, confronts his mother and father, faces the judge
and the jury and his conscience. Did he or didn't he commit
a crime? Does it matter in the end? How will he distinguish
himself from the co-defendants (who have all cut deals with
the prosecution) in the eyes of the jury? A deeply moving, fast
read that includes so many (too many) familiar scenarios from
American streets and courtrooms.

◻ *Rats Saw God* (1996)
by Rob Thomas

*"I swear, you are the only person
I know who makes decisions based on what will
provide the best material for a diary."*

••••••

From the creator of the quirky teen noir television series *Veronica Mars* comes this novel about Steve York, a former straight-A genius turned smartass who's been smoking so much weed that he might not graduate from high school. Steve must write a 100-page paper in order to graduate on time, so he decides to write about his life since high school began, from dealing with his parents' divorce to his first love (and loss). This one is full of wit and 1990s references!

Squashed (1992)
by Joan Bauer

"Not all vegetables are this draining. Lettuce doesn't bring heartache. Turnips don't ask for your soul. Potatoes don't care where you are or even where they are. Tomatoes cuddle up to anyone who'll give them mulch and sunshine."

• • • • • •

Sixteen-year-old Ellie wants to get noticed and she has two goals in mind to make it happen: 1) grow the biggest pumpkin in Iowa, and 2) lose twenty pounds. This coming-of-age tale is 100 percent funny with just the right amount of sentiment to make you shed one or two tears and root like hell for Ellie.

Stargirl (2000)
by Jerry Spinelli

"She laughed when there was no joke. She danced when there was no music. She had no friends, yet she was the friendliest person in school."

• • • • • •

Stargirl is hands down my favorite literary character of all time, and despite the title of the book, she's not even the main character—a boy named Leo Borlock is. Leo hears about the new student at his high school before he actually meets her because her reputation as a ukulele-playing, dancing, uniquely clad, strange, fearless girl precedes her. Vibrant, memorable, sensitive, beautiful Stargirl. She reminds me of my incredibly unique niece, Zinnia, who has a heart full of love to give.

What I Saw and How I Lied (2008)
by Judy Blundell

"So that's how we were: a mother and a daughter sitting on a porch, laughing as the tree shadows stretched toward the porch and lights came on in the houses. Sounds cozy. But it was just like buzz bombs—the V-2 rockets the Germans launched at London near the end of the war. You couldn't hear them, not even a whistle. Until your house blew up."

• • • • • •

Part mystery, part historical fiction, this book is set in 1947 America and revolves around part-girl, part-woman Evie, whose stepdad is back from the war and takes her and her mom on an extended trip to Florida without much in the way of an explanation. That's where Evie meets Peter Coleridge and everything changes. Catapulted into adulthood, where things are complicated and the truth is shrouded in lies, Evie is me, Evie is every teenage girl who wants to grow up without really knowing what it entails.

Appendix

Master Checklist

- [ ] *84, Charing Cross Road* (1970) by Helene Hanff
- [ ] *The Absolutely True Diary of a Part-Time Indian* (2007) by Sherman Alexie
- [ ] *The Accident Man* (2007) by Tom Cain, read by John Lee
- [ ] *Almost Like Being in Love* (2004) by Steve Kluger
- [ ] *An Age of License: A Travelogue* (2014) by Lucy Knisley
- [ ] *American Gods* (2001) by Neil Gaiman
- [ ] *The Art of Racing in the Rain* (2008) by Garth Stein
- [ ] *The Art of the Steal* (2004) by Christopher Mason
- [ ] *August: Osage County* (2007) by Tracy Letts
- [ ] *The Awakening* (1899) by Kate Chopin
- [ ] *The Bad Seed* (1954) by William March
- [ ] *The Beautiful Things That Heaven Bears* (2007) by Dinaw Mengestu
- [ ] *Beauty: A Retelling of the Story of Beauty and the Beast* (1978) by Robin McKinley
- [ ] *Bee Season* (2000) by Myla Goldberg
- [ ] *Beloved* (1987) by Toni Morrison
- [ ] *The Best of Roald Dahl* (1978) by Roald Dahl

❏ *Beyond Belief: The Secret Lives of Women in Extreme Religions* (2013) by Susan Tive and Cami Ostman

❏ *The Big Con: The Story of the Confidence Man* (1940) by David W. Maurer

❏ *Black Like Me* (1961) by John Howard Griffin

❏ *Blue Pills: A Positive Love Story* (2001) by Frederik Peeters

❏ *Born Standing Up: A Comic's Life* (2007) by Steve Martin

❏ *Bossypants* (2011) by Tina Fey

❏ *The Bottoms* (2000) by Joe R. Lansdale

❏ *Brothel: Mustang Ranch and Its Women* (2001) by Alexa Albert

❏ *Calling Dr. Laura: A Graphic Memoir* (2013) by Nicole J. Georges

❏ *Cancer Vixen* (2006) by Marisa Acocella Marchetto

❏ *Cane River* (2001) by Lalita Tademy

❏ *Can't We Talk about Something More Pleasant?* (2014) by Roz Chast

❏ *Catch Me If You Can: The True Story of a Real Fake* (1980) by Frank W. Abagnale

❏ *Charlotte's Web* (1952, 1980) by E.B. White, read by the author

❏ *The Children of Men* (1992) by P.D. James

❏ *Chinese Cinderella: The True Story of an Unwanted Daughter* (1999) by Adeline Yen Mah

❏ *Chocolat* (1999) by Joanne Harris

❏ *The Chronology of Water* (2011) by Lidia Yuknavitch

❏ *The Cider House Rules* (1985) by John Irving

❏ *Cold Hands, Warm Heart* (2009) by Jill Wolfson

❏ *The Collector* (1963) by John Fowles

- ☐ *A Confederacy of Dunces* (1980, 1997) by John Kennedy Toole, read by Barrett Whitener
- ☐ *The Confidence-Man: His Masquerade* (1857) by Herman Melville
- ☐ *The Cutting Season* (2012) by Attica Locke
- ☐ *Dangerous Liaisons* (1782) by Pierre Choderlos de Laclos
- ☐ *The Disreputable History of Frankie Landau-Banks* (2008) by E. Lockhart
- ☐ *Don't Let's Go to the Dogs Tonight: An African Childhood* (2001) by Alexandra Fuller
- ☐ *Dracula* (1897) by Bram Stoker
- ☐ *Eleanor & Park* (2012) by Rainbow Rowell
- ☐ *Ella Minnow Pea: A Progressively Lipogrammatic Epistolary Fable* (2001) by Mark Dunn
- ☐ *Every Day* (2012) by David Levithan, read by Alex McKenna
- ☐ *The Executioner's Song* (1979) by Norman Mailer
- ☐ *Expecting Adam: A True Story of Birth, Rebirth, and Everyday Magic* (1999) by Martha Beck
- ☐ *Farewell to Manzanar: A True Story of Japanese American Experience During and After the World War II Internment* (1972) by Jeanne Wakatsuki Houston and James D. Houston
- ☐ *Fences* (1983) by August Wilson
- ☐ *Flowers for Algernon* (1959) by Daniel Keyes
- ☐ *Forbidden* (2010) by Tabitha Suzuma
- ☐ *A Free Life* (2007) by Ha Jin, read by Jason Ma
- ☐ *Fried Green Tomatoes at the Whistle Stop Cafe* (1987) by Fannie Flagg
- ☐ *Full Dark, No Stars* (2010) by Stephen King

- ❐ *The Gentle Grafter* (1907) by O. Henry
- ❐ *Geography Club* (2003) by Brent Hartinger
- ❐ *Ghostman* (2013) by Roger Hobbs, read by Jake Weber
- ❐ *A Girl Named Zippy: Growing Up Small in Mooreland, Indiana* (2001) by Haven Kimmel
- ❐ *The Girl with the Dragon Tattoo* (2005) by Stieg Larsson
- ❐ *Give Me My Father's Body: The Life of Minik, the New York Eskimo* (1986) by Kenn Harper
- ❐ *The Godfather* (1969) by Mario Puzo
- ❐ *González and Daughter Trucking Co.: A Road Novel with Literary License* (2005) by María Amparo Escandón
- ❐ *The Good Lord Bird* (2013) by James McBride, read by Michael Boatman
- ❐ *The Good Thief* (2008) by Hannah Tinti
- ❐ *Griffin and Sabine: An Extraordinary Correspondence* (1991) by Nick Bantock
- ❐ *The Grifters* (1963) by Jim Thompson
- ❐ *A Grown-Up Kind of Pretty* (2012) by Joshilyn Jackson
- ❐ *The Gum Thief* (2007) by Douglas Coupland
- ❐ *The Haunting of Alaizabel Cray* (2001) by Chris Wooding
- ❐ *The Heart Is a Lonely Hunter* (1940) by Carson McCullers
- ❐ *Hell at the Breech* (2003) by Tom Franklin
- ❐ *High Fidelity* (1995) by Nick Hornby
- ❐ *The Hotel New Hampshire* (1981) by John Irving
- ❐ *House of Sand and Fog* (1999) by Andre Dubus III
- ❐ *The House on Mango Street* (1984) by Sandra Cisneros
- ❐ *How to Be a Heroine: Or, What I've Learned from Reading Too Much* (2014) by Samantha Ellis

- ❐ *How to Breathe Underwater* (2003) by Julie Orringer
- ❐ *How to Understand Israel in 60 Days or Less* (2010) by Sarah Glidden
- ❐ *Hyperbole and a Half: Unfortunate Situations, Flawed Coping Mechanisms, Mayhem, and Other Things That Happened* (2013) by Allie Brosh
- ❐ *Hypocrite in a Pouffy White Dress: Tales of Growing Up Groovy and Clueless* (2005) by Susan Jane Gilman
- ❐ *The Idiot Girls' Action-Adventure Club: True Tales from a Magnificent and Clumsy Life* (2002) by Laurie Notaro
- ❐ *If on a Winter's Night a Traveler* (1979) by Italo Calvino
- ❐ *The Importance of Being Earnest, A Trivial Comedy for Serious People* (1895) by Oscar Wilde
- ❐ *In the Time of the Butterflies* (1994) by Julia Alvarez
- ❐ *The Internet Is a Playground: Irreverent Correspondences of an Evil Online Genius* (2011) by David Thorne
- ❐ *Interpreter of Maladies* (1999) by Jhumpa Lahiri
- ❐ *Invisible* (2009) by Paul Auster
- ❐ *The Invisible Bridge* (2010) by Julie Orringer
- ❐ *Isadora Duncan: A Graphic Biography* (2008) by Sabrina Jones
- ❐ *It Gets Better: Coming Out, Overcoming Bullying, and Creating a Life Worth Living* (2011) by Dan Savage and Terry Miller
- ❐ *Jellicoe Road* (2006) by Melina Marchetta
- ❐ *Jesus Land* (2005) by Julia Scheeres
- ❐ *Johnny Got His Gun* (1939) by Dalton Trumbo
- ❐ *King Dork* (2006) by Frank Portman

❏ *Kissing the Witch: Old Tales in New Skins* (1997) by Emma Donoghue

❏ *Knockemstiff* (2008) by Donald Ray Pollock

❏ *Labyrinths: Selected Stories and Other Writings* (1962) by Jorge Luis Borges

❏ *Ladies and Gentlemen* (2011) by Adam Ross

❏ *Last Night at the Lobster* (2007) by Stewart O'Nan

❏ *Let's Explore Diabetes with Owls* (2013) by David Sedaris

❏ *Letters from a Nut* (1997) by Ted L. Nancy

❏ *The Lies of Locke Lamora* (2006) by Scott Lynch

❏ *Little Failure* (2014) by Gary Shteyngart

❏ *Look Me in the Eye: My Life with Asperger's* (2007) by John Elder Robison

❏ *Lost in the City* (1992) by Edward P. Jones

❏ *The Lover's Dictionary* (2010) by David Levithan

❏ *Lucky* (1999) by Alice Sebold

❏ *The Man Who Mistook His Wife for a Hat and Other Clinical Tales* (1985) by Oliver Sacks

❏ *Man's Search for Meaning* (1946) by Viktor E. Frankl

❏ *The Mark Inside: A Perfect Swindle, a Cunning Revenge, and a Small History of the Big Con* (2012) by Amy Reading

❏ *Matchstick Men: A Novel about Grifters with Issues* (2002) by Eric Garcia

❏ *Maus I: A Survivor's Tale: My Father Bleeds History* (1986) by Art Spiegelman

❏ *MemoraBEALEia: A Private Scrapbook about Edie Beale of Grey Gardens, First Cousin to First Lady Jacqueline Kennedy Onassis* (2008) by Walter Newkirk

- ❏ *Midnight in the Garden of Good and Evil* (1994) by John Berendt
- ❏ *Miss Pettigrew Lives for a Day* (1938) by Winifred Watson
- ❏ *Monster* (1999) by Walter Dean Myers
- ❏ *Mop Men: Inside the World of Crime Scene Cleaners* (2004) by Alan Emmins
- ❏ *Motherless Brooklyn* (1999, 2001) by Jonathan Lethem, read by Frank Muller
- ❏ *Mr. Penumbra's 24-Hour Bookstore* (2012) by Robin Sloan
- ❏ *Mudbound* (2008) by Hillary Jordan
- ❏ *My Heart Laid Bare* (1998) by Joyce Carol Oates
- ❏ *My Year of Meats* (1998) by Ruth L. Ozeki
- ❏ *The Namesake* (2003) by Jhumpa Lahiri
- ❏ *Nickel and Dimed: On (Not) Getting By in America* (2001) by Barbara Ehrenreich
- ❏ *On Such a Full Sea* (2014) by Chang-rae Lee, read by B.D. Wong
- ❏ *Ordinary People* (1976) by Judith Guest
- ❏ *Orientation and Other Stories* (2011) by Daniel Orozco
- ❏ *Out Stealing Horses* (2003, 2008) by Per Petterson, read by Richard Poe
- ❏ *Outer Dark* (1968) by Cormac McCarthy
- ❏ *The Outlaw Album: Stories* (2011) by Daniel Woodrell
- ❏ *The Outsiders* (1967) by S.E. Hinton
- ❏ *Outwitting History: The Amazing Adventures of a Man Who Rescued a Million Yiddish Books* (2004) by Aaron Lansky
- ❏ *Parlor Games* (2013) by Maryka Biaggio
- ❏ *Passing* (1929) by Nella Larsen

- ❐ *Persepolis: The Story of a Childhood* (2000, 2007) by Marjane Satrapi
- ❐ *The Poet Slave of Cuba: A Biography of Juan Francisco Manzano* (2006) by Margarita Engle
- ❐ *The Polysyllabic Spree* (2004) by Nick Hornby
- ❐ *PostSecret: Extraordinary Confessions from Ordinary Lives* (2005) by Frank Warren
- ❐ *Primates: The Fearless Science of Jane Goodall, Dian Fossey, and Biruté Galdikas* (2013) by Jim Ottaviani and Maris Wicks
- ❐ *The Principles of Uncertainty* (2007) by Maira Kalman
- ❐ *The Prize Winner of Defiance, Ohio* (2001) by Terry Ryan
- ❐ *Prodigal Summer* (2000) by Barbara Kingsolver, read by the author
- ❐ *Push* (1996) by Sapphire
- ❐ *The Quiet American* (1955) by Graham Greene
- ❐ *A Quiet Belief in Angels* (2007) by R.J. Ellory
- ❐ *Radioactive: Marie & Pierre Curie: A Tale of Love and Fallout* (2010) by Lauren Redniss
- ❐ *The Rape of Nanking: The Forgotten Holocaust of World War II* (1997) by Iris Chang
- ❐ *Rats Saw God* (1996) by Rob Thomas
- ❐ *Reading Lolita in Tehran: A Memoir in Books* (2003) by Azar Nafisi
- ❐ *The Reading Promise: My Father and the Books We Shared* (2011) by Alice Ozma
- ❐ *Requiem for a Dream* (1978) by Hubert Selby Jr.
- ❐ *Revolutionary Road* (1961) by Richard Yates
- ❐ *The Rise and Fall of Great Powers* (2014) by Tom Rachman
- ❐ *The Road* (2006) by Cormac McCarthy

- ☐ *Room* (2010) by Emma Donoghue, read by various readers
- ☐ *Runaway: Stories* (2004) by Alice Munro
- ☐ *S.* (2013) by Doug Dorst (created by J.J. Abrams)
- ☐ *Schindler's List* (1982) by Thomas Keneally
- ☐ *The Secret Life of the Lonely Doll: The Search for Dare Wright* (2004) by Jean Nathan
- ☐ *Serena* (2008) by Ron Rash
- ☐ *The Shadow of the Wind* (2001) by Carlos Ruiz Zafón
- ☐ *The Shiniest Jewel: A Family Love Story* (2008) by Marian Henley
- ☐ *The Shipping News* (1993) by Annie Proulx
- ☐ *Sh*t My Dad Says* (2010) by Justin Halpern
- ☐ *Sickened: The Memoir of a Munchausen by Proxy Childhood* (2003) by Julie Gregory
- ☐ *Squashed* (1992) by Joan Bauer
- ☐ *Stargirl* (2000) by Jerry Spinelli
- ☐ *Stiff: The Curious Lives of Human Cadavers* (2003) by Mary Roach
- ☐ *Stitches: A Memoir* (2009) by David Small
- ☐ *The Storied Life of A.J. Fikry* (2014) by Gabrielle Zevin
- ☐ *The Swerve: How the World Became Modern* (2011) by Stephen Greenblatt
- ☐ *Tell the Wolves I'm Home* (2012) by Carol Rifka Brunt
- ☐ *Then We Came to the End* (2007) by Joshua Ferris
- ☐ *They Marched Into Sunlight: War and Peace, Vietnam and America, October 1967* (2003) by David Maraniss
- ☐ *Three Little Words: A Memoir* (2008) by Ashley Rhodes-Courter

❑ *The Time Traveler's Wife* (2003) by Audrey Niffenegger
❑ *Tiny Beautiful Things: Advice on Love and Life from Dear Sugar* (2012) by Cheryl Strayed, read by the author
❑ *To Kill a Mockingbird* (1960) by Harper Lee
❑ *True Grit* (1968) by Charles Portis
❑ *Twelfth Night; or, What You Will* (1623) by William Shakespeare
❑ *Typical American* (1991) by Gish Jen
❑ *The Uncommon Reader* (2007) by Alan Bennett
❑ *Vanished* (2009, 2010) by Joseph Finder, read by Holter Graham
❑ *A Walk on the Wild Side* (1956) by Nelson Algren
❑ *The Warmth of Other Suns: The Epic Story of America's Great Migration* (2010) by Isabel Wilkerson
❑ *Water for Elephants* (2006) by Sara Gruen
❑ *We Wish to Inform You That Tomorrow We Will Be Killed with Our Families: Stories from Rwanda* (1998) by Philip Gourevitch
❑ *What I Saw and How I Lied* (2008) by Judy Blundell
❑ *The Wild Trees: A Story of Passion and Daring* (2007) by Richard Preston
❑ *Winter's Bone* (2006) by Daniel Woodrell
❑ *Wise Blood* (1952) by Flannery O'Connor
❑ *A Woman of Independent Means* (1978) by Elizabeth Forsythe Hailey
❑ *The Women of Brewster Place* (1982) by Gloria Naylor
❑ *World War Z: An Oral History of the Zombie War* (2006, 2014) by Max Brooks, read by various readers

- [ ] *The Worst Hard Time: The Untold Story of Those Who Survived the Great American Dust Bowl* (2006) by Timothy Egan
- [ ] *A Yellow Raft in Blue Water* (1987) by Michael Dorris
- [ ] *Yes Man* (2005) by Danny Wallace
- [ ] *Youth in Revolt: The Journals of Nick Twisp* (1993) by C.D. Payne

About the Author

Gina Sheridan is a librarian and the author of *I Work at a Public Library: A Collection of Crazy Stories from the Stacks*. When she's not reading or collecting stories, she's exploring cemeteries, dressing up her cats, or taking pictures of things overlooked by regular people. She lives in Old North St. Louis with her husband Travis. Gina can be found online at *www.ginasheridan.com*.